RADIO CONTROL MODEL HELICOPTER HANDBOOK

BY DON LODGE

TAB TAB BOOKS Inc.
BLUE RIDGE SUMMIT. PA. 17214

To my wife, Lois, for her constant encouragement, and to John Minasian, for his skill in flying the Cheyenne.

FIRST EDITION

FIRST PRINTING

Copyright © 1983 by TAB BOOKS Inc.

Printed in the United States of America

Library of Congress Cataloging in Publication Data

Lodge, Don.
    Radio control model helicopter handbook.

    Includes index.
    1. Helicopters—Models—Radio control.   I. Title.
TL776.L63   1983   629.133'1352   82-19388
ISBN 0-8306-1509-1 (pbk.)

Contents

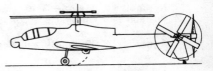

Introduction

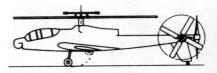

Someone once said, "There are very few machines when compared to the helicopter, pound for pound, which have more parts that rotate, oscillate, flap, wriggle, jiggle, slide, slip, vibrate, shake, rattle, twist, or flop! He was probably correct. Yet the helicopter is indeed an intriguing machine, the most efficient heavier-than-air vertical lifting device so far invented.

Radio-controlled (or R/C as we say) helicopters are here to stay. This book, therefore, will assist the serious R/C helicopter modeler in achieving a better understanding of the "whys and hows" of rotor behavior. For the more adventuresome who would like to experiment with different configurations, a section also has been included which describes and assesses, in general terms, the predominate rotor configurations which, at one time or another, have been used with some of the more obvious characteristics, advantages and disadvantages of each.

As with any subject, particularly if it's relatively new or not fully understood, the world of R/C helicopters has a sizable crop of myths, misconceptions, fashionable theories, and just plain incorrect ideas which seem to thrive. I would like to dispel some of these and explain others in the interest of the hobby in general and of the R/C helicopter model builders in particular.

General construction practices are also offered, some of which may not represent the optimum plateau of perfection. Nevertheless they are practical and reliable methods, particularly to get the novice R/C helicopter modeler started.

Several appendices are included. One provides the more ambitious and mathematically inclined reader with a procedure to follow in rotor design and also a relatively simple method of rapidly calculating (estimating would be more correct) the hover performance one might expect from any given model being considered. Another summarizes classical examples of how to calculate stresses in some of the more critical design areas, i.e., parts likely to be under high load operating conditions.

Chapter 1

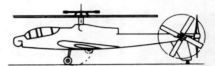

The Hovering Rotor

Let's begin by considering some of the more important things that happen to a typical blade which is part of a rotor assembly. For the moment we will not concern ourselves with the details of the rest of this assembly, but only with what this typical blade experiences and how it responds as it rotates about the shaft (or *mast* as it is usually called). Figure 1-1 is a sketch of such a blade. This blade must produce lift just as a wing does for our fixed-wing models. Beyond this, the blade has very little in common with the wing.

Let's view this same blade from the top as it rotates to produce lift in a hovering flight condition in Fig. 1-2. By the way, the "o" in hover is pronounced as in "love," *not* as in "Hoover" or "rover."

Several things are immediately apparent. For example, the part of the blade at B—B has a much higher speed through the air than the section at A—A because in one revolution B—B travels a much greater circumferential distance than the section at A—A but in the same elapsed time. The section at B—B therefore produces much more lift than at A—A. There are very sophisticated mathematical equations which would show that the spanwise distribution of lift for our untwisted, constant chord rotor blade would look something like that in Fig. 1-3. This is the same blade in Fig. 1-2, but now viewed edgewise.

Notice that lift distribution doesn't increase toward the tip as a straight line, as you might expect, but it increases as an ever-steepening curve. This is because the lift produced at any blade

1

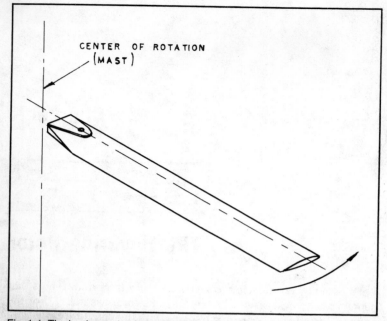

CENTER OF ROTATION
(MAST)

Fig. 1-1. The basic rotating helicopter blade. Seems simple enough, doesn't it?

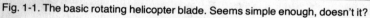

station is a function of the square of the velocity at that station.

Also note that the peak is rounded off due to *tip loss,* as some of the high pressure air under the tip spills around the end to destroy the lift on the top.

One important point to note is that if the area (shaded) under the lift curve is divided into two equal areas by a vertical line, the line would represent the "average" point where all the lift could be concentrated. We can call this point the *spanwise center of lift,* and for our untwisted, constant chord, hovering rotor blade, it is located at approximately .75R, or three-quarters of the way out from the center to the tip.

CENTRIFUGAL FORCE

Another basic aspect of our rotating blade is that, since it has weight (perhaps three to five ounces), it experiences *centrifugal force* which tends to throw it out from the axis of rotation. Don't be lulled into a false sense of security by the light weight. Centrifugal force is proportional to the weight, the square of the rotational speed (i.e., the angular velocity times itself), and the distance from the axis of rotation to what is called the *center of percussion.* You all

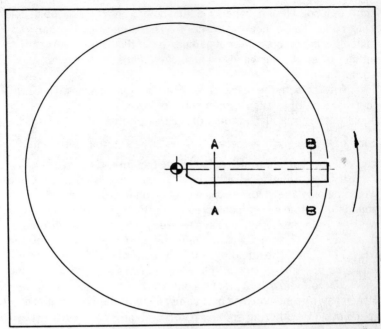

Fig. 1-2. The same blade from the top view. Notice the section at B-B is traveling much faster than the one at A-A. This is because B-B travels a much farther distance than A-A in the same time.

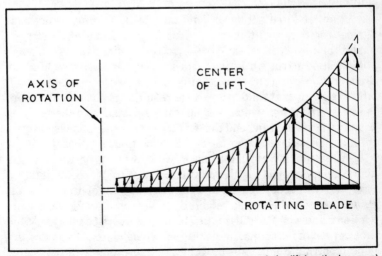

Fig. 1-3. Because lift is a function of the velocity squared, the lift (vertical arrows) does not increase at the same rate toward the tip, but increases at an ever-increasing rate.

know that solid feeling when you hit a home run with a baseball bat. Your hands feel almost no reaction. That's because the ball contacted the bat at this center of percussion. If the ball contacts the bat either closer to your hands or near the end of the bat, your hands sting, don't they?

Now, back to the blade. If the chord is constant (spanwise) and there are no tip weights, the center of percussion of the blade is equal to the total blade radius (mast to tip) divided by the square root of 3 or $\frac{R}{\sqrt{3}} = \frac{R}{1.73}$. If you browse through Appendix C you will see that when each of the above quantities is converted into compatible mathematical units, centrifugal force on a rotating blade weighing only a few ounces can easily be on the order of 150 to 200 pounds. It should be reemphasized that rotating blades (tail rotor as well as main rotor) are subject to tremendous forces and must, therefore, be regarded with *caution* and *prudence!* I always cringe when I see someone standing in the tip-path-plane of a rotating tail rotor, or sighting along the plane of a main rotor for a tracking check. If you *must* do it, make your visit of very short duration; blades have been known to part company with the hub at full rotor speed due to feathering-spindle bolt metal fatigue. (I have experienced two!)

DRAG

Another force acting on our rotor blade is *drag,* which acts against rotation, and the drag vector is *always* in a plane at right angles (or *normal* as we say), to the axis of rotation. We have a small complication here. All lifting blades or airfoils have two kinds of drag, or drag arising from two sources. First, we have *induced drag,* which is an inherent and inseparable result of producing lift. There is also *profile drag,* which is simply the resistance to the blade in parting the viscous air, and the skin friction as the blade is dragged through the viscous air in the no-lift condition.

At this point we will introduce two new terms pertinent to the above. *Induced power* is the power required to overcome induced drag, which of course exists inherently as a result of producing lift. *Profile power* is the power required to overcome profile drag (skin friction if you wish) on the rotating blade at zero lift condition. At the proper time these terms, or quantities, will fall into place and will, I hope, contribute much to the general picture of why a helicopter rotor behaves as it does.

4

AIRFOILS

We've discussed the major forces that act on a rotating blade, i.e., lift, centrifugal force, and drag, but so far nothing has been said about the blade shape. Just how important is the airfoil shape to the performance of an R/C helicopter? To answer this question a new term must be briefly discussed. This term is the Reynolds Number (N_R).

This is a dimensionless ratio that defines the relative state of the airflow around any airfoil in terms of the airfoil chord length, velocity of the air, density, and viscosity of the air. Small wings moving at low speed have a low N_R (40,000—50,000 for a rubber-powered model), and large wings moving at high speed have very high N_R (6 to 8 million, written as 8×10^6).

At the low N_R range, airfoil shape is not too important; most any shape within reason is satisfactory. At the high N_R range, the shape of the airfoil is very critical in achieving the desired characteristics. Most of our R/C model rotor blades operate (near the tip at least) at N_R of from approximately 250,000 to 500,000 and it so happens that this is within the general range of N_R that the shape of an airfoil *does* begin to be effective in the performance of a rotor. For what it's worth, you can calculate the tip speed of your rotor as shown in Appendix A under N_R.

If we have a general idea of what characteristics make up a good airfoil for an R/C helicopter, then we can look for these among the published wind-tunnel data available. The principal characteristics are:

☐ Slope of the lift curve ($\dfrac{dC_L}{d\alpha}$).
☐ Stall angle (in the N_R range of our models).
☐ Lift-to-drag ratio (L/D).
☐ Pitching moment versus angle of attack, i.e., center of pressure travel (CP).

Well, we can forget the first characteristic since all airfoils have about the same slope of the curve. Is stall angle important? Maybe, but I have yet to see an R/C helicopter stall. I know it's currently fashionable to talk about retreating tip stall, but it just doesn't occur—at least, with the models to date. (This is covered in detail in Chapter 6.)

Lift-do-drag ratio is significant, even at the N_R our blades are operating. In the case of fixed-wing machines, usually the *maximum* L/D (and the corresponding angle of attack), is all that is important because the fixed-wing machine, except during landing or a sharp maneuver, seldom strays far from that maximum L/D by design. The helicopter rotor blade, by contrast, in level cruise flight varies in angle of attack from about -2 to about $+6$ or 7 degrees once each rotor revolution! It is important, then, to select an airfoil that maintains low drag throughout the range of, say -3 to $+9$ degrees or so.

Pitching moment, or center of pressure travel, is also important at our rotor blade N_R, because an excessive (CP) excursion, with angle of attack change, can inject unwanted blade feathering changes that can result in erratic cyclic pitch or roll behavior. This is particularly true if the control system is "spongy," as we say.

So what kind of airfoil do we look for? In general the classes of airfoils that meet the above requirements are (1) the symmetrical sections including the NACA (00) series (0012 or 0015) or the NACA (230) series (23012 or 23015*), and (2) the semi-symmetrical sections of which the NACA M6 is one of the best. It has a good L/D at low or negative angles of attack. I know of no full-size machine that uses a flat bottom section such as the Clark Y or variations on this theme. They are, however, certainly easier to carve for our models and maybe that's justification enough, at least for the present.

So far we have studied a single rotor blade as it rotates, and we have discussed lift, drag, centrifugal force, and airfoil aerodynamic pitching moments about the feathering axis. Now let's consider a complete rotor with two blades rotating and developing lift in a hover. Figure 1-4 is such a rotor.

For the time being we will say the blades are untwisted, constant chord, and that the blades are fully articulated, i.e., hinged so that they are free to flap up and down, are hinged to permit *in-plane motion* (called *lead-lag*), and *feather* (change pitch) about the 25% chord. If the feathering of the blades is coordinated to occur both equally and in the *same direction,* then the control is called *collective pitch.* If the feathering is equal, but one *positive* while the other *negative*, then the control is called *cyclic pitch.* We will not concern ourselves with the mechanics of the rotor at this point.

ROTOR CONING

The first thing we will consider in our hovering rotor of Fig. 1-4

---

*The 12 and 15 refer to the ratio (in percent) of thickness to chord.

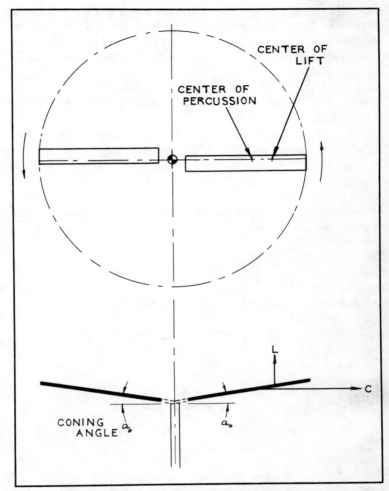

Fig. 1-4. Top and side view of a lifting rotor. The side view shows two important forces that act on a lifting rotor. They are lift (L) and centrifugal force (CF). If the blade is free to flap (like a bird), then the combination of L and CF determine the coning angle a_o.

is the coning angle. What is it? Is it important? If so, how can we predict what it will be?

Coning is the angle between a plane normal to the axis of no feathering (same as rotational axis in our hovering rotor) and the blade. It is formed by the equilibrium between the lift moment and the centrifugal moment on the blade. From Fig. 1-2 and its accompanying discussion on lift and centrifugal force, we know that for an untwisted, constant chord blade, the lift can be considered to be concentrated at .75R (or three fourths of the way from the hub to the tip). From the same section, we know that centrifugal force can be very high and that it acts at a distance $\frac{R}{1.73}$ from the center. Figure 1-5 considers one blade of this rotor in detail with the coning angle exaggerated a bit for clarity.

Let's calculate the centrifugal force for a typical blade. The formula for centrifugal force (CF) is as follows:

$$CF = \frac{w}{g} \Omega^2 \sqrt{\frac{R}{3}}$$

Now don't let this scare you; we'll go through it step by step together.

$$CF = \frac{w}{g} \Omega^2 \sqrt{\frac{R}{3}}$$

$$CF = \left(\frac{.25}{32.2}\right)(136)^2(1.11)$$

$$CF = (.007764)(18523)(1.11)$$

$$CF = 160 \text{ lbs}$$

where

w = weight of blade in pounds (assume 4 oz = .25 pounds)

g = acceleration of gravity = 32.2 ft/sec²

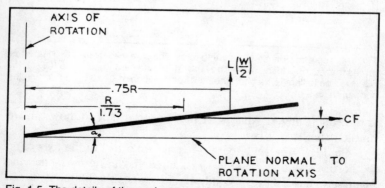

Fig. 1-5. The details of the coning are clearly shown here. First find CF, then solve for Y as detailed in the text.

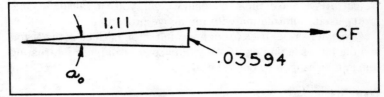

Fig. 1-6. In this illustration, a_o turns out to be not quite two degrees.

Ω = angular velocity of rotor in radians per second = $\dfrac{RPM \times 2\pi}{60}$

RPM = angular speed of rotor in revolutions per minute (assume 1300 RPM here)

so: $\Omega = \dfrac{1300 \times 2\pi}{60} = 136 \dfrac{radians}{sec}$

(π = 3.14-constant)

assume R = 23 inches = 1.92 feet therefore $\dfrac{R}{1.73}$ = 1.11 ft. where $\sqrt{3}$ = 1.73

This blade will seek the coning angle that will put the moments due to lift and centrifugal force in equilibrium, such that, referring to Fig. 1-5, (CF) (Y) = (L) (.75R). Assuming the helicopter weighs 8 pounds, each blade, therefore, lifts 4 pounds. The equation becomes: $(160)(Y) = (4) (.75) (1.92)$. Solving for Y, $Y = \dfrac{5.75}{160}$ = .036 feet (or about .4 inches). Now let's redraw Fig. 1-5 using just the parts we need to find the coning angle (denoted as a_o), (Fig. 1-6).

We know $\dfrac{R}{\sqrt{3}}$ = 1.11 and we just calculated (Y) to be .036 feet. Now if we ratio $\dfrac{.036}{1.11}$, this is called the *sine* of the angle a_o. Therefore: sine $a_o = \dfrac{.036}{1.11}$ = .0323.

Conveniently for us, the sine of a small angle (up to about 3 degrees), in trigonometry, is approximately equal to the angle itself expressed in *radians*. Since coning angles seldom exceed 3 degrees, we are home free. Therefore, when the sine of a_o = .0323, we can say that the angle equals .0323 radians. Because a radian equals 57.3 degrees, then a_o = (.0323) (57.3) = 1.85 degrees coning. In other words, this particular rotor has a coning angle of a little less than two degrees. If you know the values for the blade

9

weight, RPM, and estimated model weight, you can calculate some pretty useful information with the above procedure.

Now let's refer back to our hovering rotor and look at the airfoil and the forces acting on it. We will uncover still more interesting things that happen to our rotating blade.

MASS BALANCE

By definition, lift always acts *normal* (at right angles) to the airflow, and drag always acts parallel to the airflow. Figure 1-7 is a typical helicopter blade with the lift and drag acting from the center of pressure. It would be downright clever to position the *feather axis* (the point about which the blade will be mechanically rotated to change collective or cyclic pitch) at the center of pressure. Aerodynamically, this would provide a neutrally stable pitching moment characteristic—or in other words, no twisting force—right? Well, it sounds great, but it doesn't quite work out that way. First, no matter how hard we try to reproduce any desired airfoil, there will always be discrepancies, little variations here and there. Our particular blades may want to pitch up or down, and may therefore be candidates for flutter.

Let's get some idea of what this flutter instability is, what causes it, and how we can prevent it. Consider the airfoil in Fig. 1-8, which is a repeat of Fig. 1-7 except that the center of gravity position has been added in an unfavorable position which would aggravate flutter.

First, we know that when objects are projected freely through the air, they always tend to rotate so that the center of gravity leads the center of pressure. What would an arrow do if the weight was shifted from the point to a location near the feather? It would try to swap ends! The airfoil in Fig. 1-8, we will assume, is attached to the

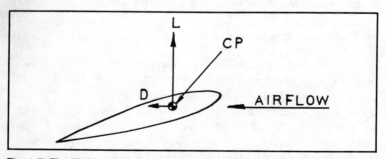

Fig. 1-7. The lift (L) and drag (D) always act at the center of pressure and are *always* normal and parallel, respectively, to the air flow direction.

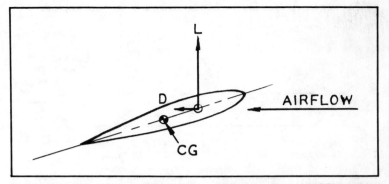

Fig. 1-8. The same blade as in Fig. 1-7 except the center of gravity (CG) is behind the center of pressure (CP). This blade would be unstable; that is, it would flutter and probably destroy itself.

hub at the feathering axis so as to restrain feathering. If you grasp the tip and tried to feather the blade, the restraint would hold but the blade would deflect like a torsional spring, the degree of rotational deflection being a function of your applied torque and the relative rigidity of the blade material.

Now let's whirl this blade rapidly and see what happens. It's pretty obvious that this blade, due to the relative positions of the lift and drag (CP), and the center of gravity (CG), is going to try to twist nose-up in an attempt to position the CG ahead of the CP, and will deflect until the dynamic moment is equal to but opposing the torsional spring moment in the blade. Having relatively low damping, the blade tip reaches the maximum angle and then "bounces" torsionally back the other way. Now the CG will try to "pass" the CP, causing a nose-down dynamic moment—again, until it reaches the spring limit of the blade and bounces back the other way again, completing one cycle of *flutter*. It is not at all uncommon for the above to occur many times a second—in fact, so rapidly that it can scarcely be seen. Depending on the relative magnitude of the various parameters including particularily the center of gravity position and blade torsional stiffness, the flutter magnitude can be anything from merely an annoying vibration and the source of excessive wear to total destruction during a rapidly diverging amplitude.

Years and dollars worth of experience has taught us that our airfoil, imperfect as it may be, *can* be made quite stable in pitch (i.e., avoid flutter) by prudent consideration of where the blade mass (weight) is relative to the best estimate of the location of the center of pressure. *How's that again?* Very simply put, the blade

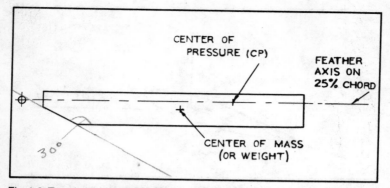

Fig. 1-9. Top view of an unstable blade. To be stable and not flutter, the CG must be on or ahead of the CP.

should balance chordwise on or slightly forward of the 25% chord point. Consider Fig. 1-9. The airfoil in Fig. 1-7 would probably be unstable because the CG is behind the CP. Blades shaped from a single piece of wood may very well end up like Fig. 1-7, because although the trailing edge is thin and the CG may be forward of the 50% chord, it seldom is near the 25% chord point. I tend to favor blades using a white oak leading edge and a balsa trailing edge. They are a lot more work, but oak leading edges move the blade center of gravity forward, and the oak also provides an excellent spar that resists bending and torsion. This blade would look something like Fig. 1-10.

Suggestions on fabricating such a blade are in Chapter 9. Even these blades, on occasion, are margined, i.e., the CG may still be aft of the 25% point. The following is just one of several ways to determine the CG location. First, measure the blade chord and place a mark on both ends one-fourth of the way back from the

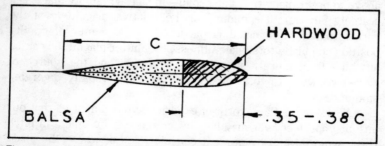

Fig. 1-10. Cross section view of a composite blade. The leading edge is a heavy hard wood such as oak, while the trailing edge is balsa. See Chapter 9 for method of construction.

12

leading edge, (25%). Using pliers, press some dressmaker's pins as accurately as possible on the 25% marks and midway between the top and bottom to form a straight feathering axis. Now obtain two straight knife edges (actually, any two pieces of metal with a straight edge will do) and hold them with C-clamps or blocks so that the edges are level. Carefully place the blade with the two pins resting on the edges. If the blade tilts nose-up, it means the center of gravity (or mass) is aft of the 25% chord as shown in Fig. 1-9. This blade is a candidate for instability.

To correct the situation, weight must be added at the leading edge to move the CG forward, thus assuring stability in pitch. The *same* amount (as nearly as possible) must be added to *each* blade in a set to keep them matched. There are several accepted methods to add mass balance. (The chordwise mass is not to be confused with balancing the *rotor assembly*. We are not ready for that just yet.) But where do we add this mass, spanwise—tip, midspan, or inboard? How do we know how much weight to add? Well, first, we know that the most efficient place, chordwise, will be right at the leading edge, or as close as possible. Wrap a piece of masking tape over the leading edge as shown in Fig. 1-11, and wrap pieces of junk lead into the tape until the blade balances, or preferably, hangs nose-down slightly. The weight should be placed about one inch from the tip, because while the dynamic balance about the feature axis is satisfied

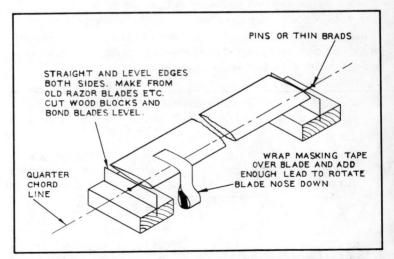

PINS OR THIN BRADS

STRAIGHT AND LEVEL EDGES BOTH SIDES. MAKE FROM OLD RAZOR BLADES ETC. CUT WOOD BLOCKS AND BOND BLADES LEVEL.

WRAP MASKING TAPE OVER BLADE AND ADD ENOUGH LEAD TO ROTATE BLADE NOSE DOWN

QUARTER CHORD LINE

Fig. 1-11. One of several ways to determine the CG location and how to determine how much weight is needed at the leading edge, if the blade is unstable.

anywhere spanwise, remember that the tips feel the highest aerodynamic loads. So the mass balance must be placed where the blade would be the most likely to flutter—that is, at the tip.

When the correct amount of lead is found that will position the CG as desired, the lead should be removed, carefully weighed, and recorded. I use an ancient letter scale that has accuracy to within roughly .1 ounce. It is not uncommon for the required added weight to be as much as half an ounce or so. Be advised that with this weight to be added to the tip, the $\frac{R}{\sqrt{3}}$ expression for the location of the center of percussion is no longer valid. There are complex mathematical ways to correct for the added weight, but the simplest way is to recalculate the blade centrifugal force based on the measured distance from the *center of rotation* to the new *spanwise* point where the blade and the installed tip weight balances on a knife edge. The newly calculated centrifugal force in which the measured distance shown in Fig. 1-12 is used in place of $\frac{R}{\sqrt{3}}$ in the formula is not absolutely accurate. The answer tends to be slightly conservative, but this is okay because the calculated load tends to come out slightly higher than the actual load. You will therefore be designing the blade hub (Appendix C) to be a little stronger than is actually required. A suggested method of attaching these mass balance weights is also discussed in Chapter 9.

One bonus fallout from having to add tip weights is that it reduces the coning angle slightly. The advantage of a small coning angle will become evident when we begin to look at our rotor, and the forces on it, in forward flight later on.

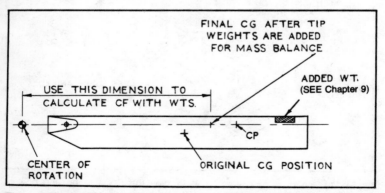

Fig. 1-12. A blade with the CG position corrected by the addition of weight at the tip.

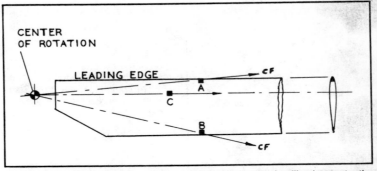

Fig. 1-13. All blades when whirled (even in a vacuum) will migrate to the knife-edge position. Notice the (CF) for each little section anywhere on the blade is on a line through the center of rotation, *not* parallel to the blade axis except for those sections positioned on the axis.

CENTRIFUGAL RESTORING MOMENT (CRM)

Sounds horrible, doesn't it? Well, it really isn't that bad. Simply stated, if any rotating blade (or, for that matter, a flat slab) is mounted so that it can feather (pitch) freely about a spanwise axis, the rotating blade (or slab) will always migrate in pitch so that it is flat, i.e., edgewise in the plane of rotation. This is true even for a symmetrical airfoil feathering about 25% chord point. Remember the discussion on airfoils? You will recall that the section concerned *aerodynamic* characteristics of the airfoil. Now we have one more item that is quite important because it results in a very strong pitching moment which acts on the blade. But you say, "you led me to believe that a symmetrical airfoil feathering about the 25% chord point had *no* pitching moment!" Would you believe that the CRM would occur even if the blade was whirling in a vacuum? It's true, because the CRM is dependent only on *dynamic* loads, whereas the discussion on airfoils was concerned with aerodynamic loads. I think you will see how it occurs in Fig. 1-13.

First, we all realize that any blade (or slab if you will) is made up of many little units of mass (or weight) which, when considered as a whole, make up the composite blade. Consider any two such units of weight located anywhere on the blade and see what happens. I've selected one on the leading edge and one on the trailing edge, and this is a valid selection because there really are two typical unit weights located there. The CF which acts on "unit masses" A and B, respectively, are on a line in a direction from the axis of rotation through A and B—not, repeat *not* parallel to the feather axis (with one exception, when the unit weight is located *on*

15

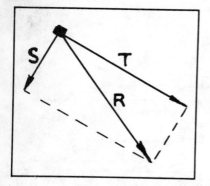

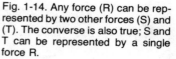

Fig. 1-14. Any force (R) can be represented by two other forces (S) and (T). The converse is also true; S and T can be represented by a single force R.

the feather axis as in C). Any two forces acting on a body at say, 90 degrees to each other, can be replaced by a single resultant force as in Fig. 1-14. Thus if component forces S and T are replaced by R, nothing is changed. Conversely, a single force R can be replaced by two components S and T and the unit mass they act on wouldn't know the difference. Now back to Fig. 1-13 (which is drawn purposely out of scale for clarity). We can replace the CF on A and on B by two components, one parallel to the blade feather axis and one 90 degrees to the blade axis as in Fig. 1-15.

The two components parallel to the blade axis have already been calculated. The *summation* of all these parallel forces acting on all of the unit masses in the entire blade has been calculated as the *centrifugal force*. We can forget these for the moment because we are interested in the other components acting at right angles to the axis and identified as A_{RM} and B_{RM}. Figure 1-16 shows these forces A_{RM} and B_{RM}. Notice that they always act in the plane of the centrifugal force field, i.e., normal to the axis of rotation. To put it

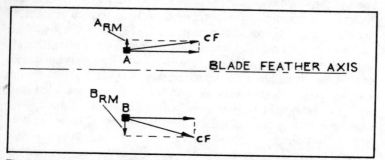

Fig. 1-15. Here, the centrifugal force on the little sections A and B in Fig. 1-13, is broken down into two forces, one parallel to the blade axis and the other normal to the axis A_{RM} and B_{RM}.

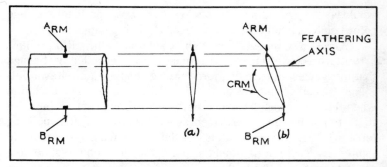

Fig. 1-16. Here only A_{RM} and B_{RM} are considered. It can be readily seen how these forces twist the blade into the knife-edge position. This is called Centrifugal Restoring Moment (CRM).

another way, if the shaft of the axis of rotation passed through a pane of glass so that the shaft was at right angles in all directions, the axis is said to be "normal" to the plane. Now look at the airfoil from the end, and you will see the forces in (a) of Fig. 1-16.

Now let's increase the blade *incidence* to a higher position at (b). It can be seen that even if this blade whirled in a vacuum at a high incidence angle, there would obviously be no lift due to the lack of air, but the two forces A_{RM} and B_{RM} form a *couple* (torque) which will tend to force the blade back down into the plane of rotation as in (a).

When we make a summation of all of the normal forces acting on all of the countless masses over the entire blade (except those on the feather axis), they will add up to a sizeable (indeed powerful), pitching moment that tends to make a blade *dynamically* seek the flat position. This is exactly what happens. The thought may occur to you that the mass balance we added a few pages back to the CG forward to 25% chord point would tend to aggravate the CRM. Actually, quite the opposite is true. Yes, we added weight at the position A in Fig. 1-12, but the net result was that by moving the CG forward to the feather axis, we were in effect removing a lot of mass unit weights from position B (or thereabouts) and relocating them on C. You may also wonder if the CRM contributes any damping effect to stop flutter. The answer is *no*. I have seen improperly designed blades flutter about the zero angle of attack position. You might think that perhaps a reflexed tab (a trailing edge tab located near the tip and bent up) would be a good way to oppose the CRM, and indeed it would tend to do that, but at the expense of high drag (power required). The most serious objection to the tab is that it would be using *aerodynamics* to correct a *dynamic* problem. Strange rotor behavior would result, particularly in high speed flight.

Back to R/C models—one simple solution to the CRM problem is to attach a coil spring somewhere in the system collective linkage that introduces an opposing force. For example, in my Kavan Jet-Ranger, a coil spring was attached to the collective plate such that when the servo was disconnected, the collective control migrated to the top of the collective system as well as providing the opposing force to CRM. The net result is less deflection in the system (due to lighter net loads) in flight and also a lighter load on the collective servo motor.

One method which has been used in the past on full size main rotors will be briefly decribed here for the record. I do *not* recommend using it on models, for although it is the purest, most straightforward solution, it can be also the most dangerous because it is subject to very high alternating loads and therefore may potentially fail unless very skillfully designed. Figure 1-17 is a sketch of the device.

When the same force components described in the discussion of Fig. 1-16 are applied to weights of Fig. 1-17, the couple developed, is trying to flatten the weights into the plane of rotation, and by so doing opposes the couple that makes up the CRM. Keep in mind that in addition to centrifugal force, these dumbell weights are subjected to very heavy alternating loads rotating about the feather axis, one cycle each rotor revolution when the machine is in forward flight. The combination of the high steady load due to CF and the

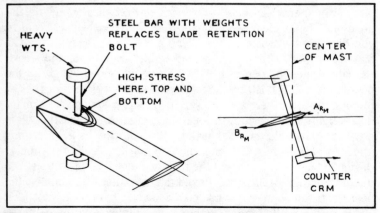

Fig. 1-17. One method (not recommended for modelers) that has been used to offset CRM.

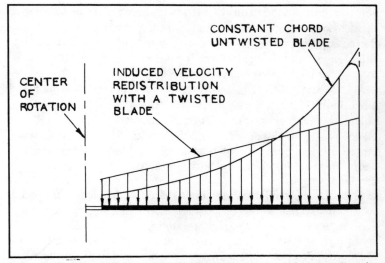

CENTER
OF
ROTATION

INDUCED VELOCITY
REDISTRIBUTION
WITH A TWISTED
BLADE

CONSTANT CHORD
UNTWISTED BLADE

Fig. 1-18. One method of increasing the efficiency of a rotor blade is reduce the high drag due to high lift at the tip. This is accomplished by twisting the blade. By twisting the tip (linear twist) 5 to 8 degrees, efficiency can be improved 4 to 5 percent.

alternating load due to feathering makes the bar a likely candidate for fatigue failure at a point (top or bottom) where the bar contacts the hub fork unless the bar is very skillfully designed. If and when it does let go, it may hit someone, and you know the rest.

The topic of centrifugal restoring moment is worthy of discussion for the modeler because he may not be aware that this phenomenon can cause high loads and undesirable deflections in the control system, as well as high loads on the servo motor.

BLADE REFINEMENTS

There are two or perhaps three refinements that can be applied to a constant chord untwisted blade that are important enough that the R/C builder should be aware of them. Each has to do with increased efficiency, i.e., developing more lift for a constant power—or conversely, requiring less power to develop the same lift. (Keep in mind we are talking *blades* here—not rotor design, yet). Let's go back to the discussion on lift and drag where we learned that *induced power* is the power necessary to overcome *induced drag*, which occurs inherently and solely as a result of producing lift. Figure 1-3 is repeated in Fig. 1-18 for convenience. We know what to do to produce lift; air must be acelerated to high velocity in the opposite direction (down). Figure 1-18 is drawn with the arrows pointing down to represent the relative magnitudes of the velocity vectors spanwise from the axis of rotation to the tip. This velocity to produce lift is called *induced velocity* and the power to produce it is called *induced power*.

Unfortunately, *lift* at any given spanwise point on the blade is a function of the square of the induced velocity or V_i^2. The induced power is a function of the cube of the induced velocity, or V_i^3! A glance at Fig. 1-18 suggests that the greatest part of the induced power is consumed by that portion of the blade nearest the tip, because here the induced velocity is greatest, and therefore, V_i^3 is tremendous.

Well, what could we do about the outer portion of the blade consuming so much power? The situation exists because the tip is traveling at the highest tangential speed and there is little we can do about that. If we could only redistribute the induced velocity more evenly over the blade, spanwise, then we could still produce the same lift but avoid those high velocities (and the V_i^3) that hurt us so badly.

One way is to build twist into the blade so that the inboard part of the blade has a higher incidence angle than the tip. The common term for this is tip *wash-out*. Linear twist (or wash-out) of up to 8 degrees is used on almost all full-sized helicopters with a saving of up to 5% induced power required. This translates to about 4.5 percent of the total power—required since induced power constitutes about 50-80 percent of the total power required to hover. One can see in Fig. 1-18 that, with blade twist, induced velocities at the tip are indeed reduced (due to lower incidence); when these lower velocities at the tip are cubed, the total induced power would be less, even though the inboard velocities are higher. The net result is that the twisted blade *is* more efficient.

You may wonder "if twist is so good, why not make it like a propeller, rather than limit it to just 8 degrees or so?" Indeed, if the rotor only hovered, it should have a high degree of twist because just as with the propeller, the incoming air would have axial flow (parallel to the axis of rotation). Our helicopter rotor, however, serves two functions—hover and forward flight where the inflow is very unsymmetrical. A twist of 5 to 8 degrees represents a fair compromise, i.e., no twist results in less efficient hover, whereas more than about 8 degrees begins to compromise forward flight efficiency.

Another way to achieve almost the same result is to build the

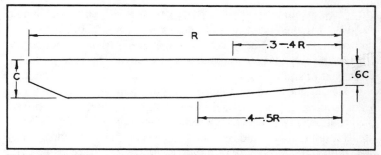

Fig. 1-19. Another way to improve efficiency is to use a tapered blade. This redistributes the lift somewhat as shown in Fig. 1-18.

blade with no twist, but with taper, either straight or perhaps as shown in Figs. 1-19 and 1-20. The tapered blade configuration is not quite as effective as the twist in reducing the induced power required, but it is easier to make. A partially tapered blade, as shown, would reduce the power required by about 4 percent. This translates to about 3.6 (or so) percent total power to hover. Unlike the twisted blade, the tapered (or partially tapered) blade does not compromise high speed flight efficiency.

The third and easiest way to improve efficiency is to reduce the profile drag (skin friction) by maintaining clean, smooth, waxed or polished blades on both main and tail rotor. Any flight test engineer will tell you that it is essential to remove all oil, dirt, bugs, etc., and present a slick, smooth finish if maximum efficiency is to be realized. For instance, an average 3000 pound helicopter can lift, with the same power, about 100 pounds more payload after all the road dirt, grit, bugs, etc., have been removed and the main and tail rotors waxed. This is an additional 3+ percent of the *total* power (induced and profile).

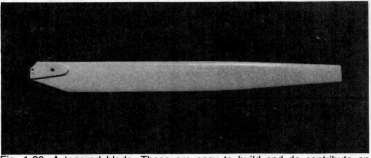

Fig. 1-20. A tapered blade. These are easy to build and do contribute an improvement in efficiency.

The bottom line is that 5—8 degree twisted, tapered, cleaned and waxed blades (main and tail rotor) can add up to about 10 percent improvement in efficiency. That is, an average 10 pound helicopter with all the above refinements would probably be able to lift an additional pound or so, using the same power setting as required without the above refinements. (I'm not so naive as to think that after reading this, there will be a mass stampede to incorporate these refinements. There may come a time in the near future when these refinements could be important in competition flying. They are, therefore, offered here as suggestions for future trends and nothing more.)

Chapter 2

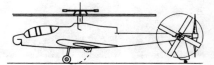

The Rotor in Forward Flight

Let's get a clear picture of a rotor blade as it rotates about the shaft, and at the same time is being subjected to forward flight (Fig. 2-1). Figure 2-2 is a top view of such a rotor. You will notice in Fig. 2-2 a symbol that looks like a little pitchfork. This is the Greek letter "psi" (ψ) and it is pronounced as "sigh." In helicopter engineering, ψ is universally used to denote the rotor azimuth (blade position around the circle). It always begins with $\psi = 0$ at the rearward position and increases in the same direction the rotor turns, and is here always expressed in degrees. Thus, the blade is rearward at $\psi = 0$ (or 360) degrees, advancing at $\psi = 90$ degrees, forward at $\psi = 180$ degrees, and the blade is "retreating" at $\psi = 270$ degrees. Referring to Fig. 2-2 it becomes obvious that the "advancing" blade at $\psi = 90$ degrees is subjected to a much higher velocity than the retreating blade at $\psi = 270$ degrees. The advancing blade feels the velocity due to rotation *plus* the velocity due to the helicopter forward speed, where as the retreating blade feels the velocity due to rotation *minus* the velocity due to forward speed. Incidently, the ratio of the helicopter velocity to the rotor tip speed is called the *advance ratio* and is denoted by the Greek letter μ (pronounced "mew"). It is approximately defined as $\dfrac{.965V}{\Omega R}$ where V is the forward velocity of the helicopter and ΩR is the tangential speed of the blade tip. The Greek letter omega (Ω) is the rational speed of the rotor in radians per second.

Fig. 2-1. The author's Lockheed Cheyenne in a gear-up high speed pass.

Lift is directly proportional to the blade angle of attack and to the velocity. Therefore, for a blade to produce the same lift, the angle of attack must necessarily be low where the net velocity is high, and high where the net velocity is low, and so we introduce *cyclic pitch*. Referring back to Fig. 2-2, α would be low at $\psi = 90$ degrees and high at $\psi = 180$ degrees. In forward flight, once each revolution each blade goes through one complete cycle—medium, to low, to medium, to high, and back to medium pitch again.

Let's lay the above concept of cyclic pitch aside for the moment and consider the problem from a different viewpoint. Figure 2-3A is a rotor that is turning and developing lift in a hover, ie., zero horizontal speed. The blades have fixed pitch (incidence angle) but are free to flap, and thus assume some coning angle (a_o) due to equilibrium between lift and centrifugal moments. The rotor lift vector is coincident with the rotational axis because the lift at all azimuth positions is the same. Now, while the rotor is turning, let's introduce a horizontal velocity. How? Well, the entire rotor and drive system could be mounted on wheels and put into motion, or the system could be stationary and a large fan started up to simulate a translatory speed. It matters not; the results basically are the same.

When the fan is started up as in Fig. 2-3B, the lifting rotor will always "flap" to produce a horizontal thrust component that is opposite from the direction of the oncoming horizontal air flow. The rotor is said to "flap back." Why does this happen? Refer to Fig. 2-2 again and recall that the velocity is higher on the advancing side at $\psi = 90$ degrees and low on the retreating side at $\psi = 270$ degrees.

24

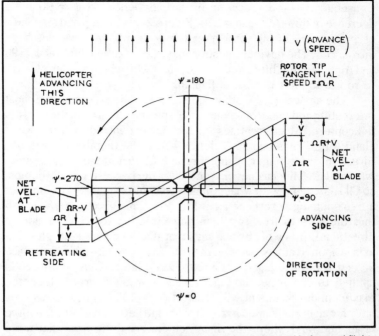

Fig. 2-2. This is the top view or a rotor (four blade) rotating and in forward flight. The rotor is rotating counterclockwise here. The advancing blade (RH) feels the speed due to rotation *plus* the forward speed. The retreating blade (LH) feels the rotational speed *minus* the forward speed.

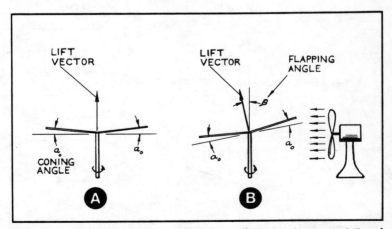

Fig. 2-3. A hovering lifting rotor (A) with coning. In B this rotor has a translation of air horizontally across it. The rotor maintains its coning, but flaps "back" or away from the oncoming air.

25

Consequently, an increase in lift is experienced at $\psi = 90$ and a decrease of lift is felt at $\psi = 270$. Figure 2-4 is the top and side view of a *fixed pitch* lifting rotor after the horizontal velocity has been introduced. The obvious question is: If the maximum lift is at $\psi = 90$ and the minimum lift is at $\psi = 270$, then why wouldn't the rotor try to roll to the left instead of flapping back?!

The answer to the above question introduces one of the most interesting and important concepts to be encountered in the study of helicopters. Most treatises on the subject introduce the "Right Hand Rule" (or some such thing) where the thumb points in one direction, index finger in another, and the rest of the fingers somewhere else. This has never worked for me because I'm all thumbs, so I'll approach it with what I think is a simple explanation. Consider a free spinning gyroscope as in Fig. 2-5. This gyro is *gimballed* so that the axis to free to tilt in any direction (or combination of directions). A law of physics says that if a force parallel to the spin axis is applied at any point on the rim, the gyro will always displace 90 degrees (or a quarter of a revolution) later! Thus, if a force is applied to the paper in Fig. 2-5 at $\psi = 90$ degrees, then the maximum displacement will occur at $\psi = 180$ (always 90 degrees later for an unrestrained gyro). This angle between where the force is applied, and where the displacement resulting from that force occurs, is called the *phase angle* of the *gyroscopic precession*.

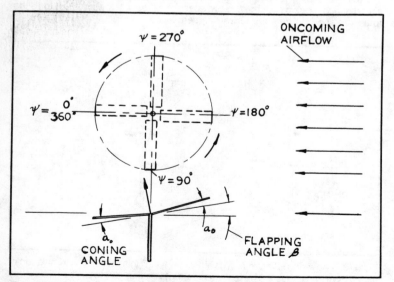

Fig. 2-4. Here the coning and flapping are shown more clearly.

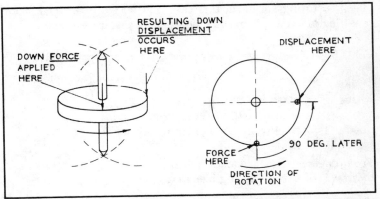

Fig. 2-5. The action of a gyroscope. If a force is applied at the rim parallel to the axis, the gyro always displaces 90 degrees later in rotation.

ROTOR BLADE PHASE ANGLE

The gyro was introduced, above, because most of us at one time or another have played with a toy gyro and are familar with the precession. Now let's discuss the application to a rotor blade. Consider a rotor blade as in Fig. 2-6. We are looking at it edgewise as it freely flaps up and down once per revolution as the rotor translates in forward flight.

As the blade displaces up and down, centrifugal force acting on the blade opposes any force tending to take the whirling blade out of a plane normal to the rotating axis. Thus it can be said that CF acts

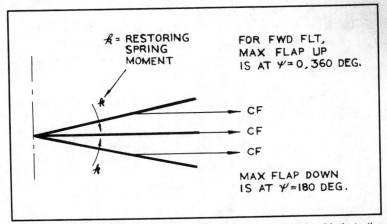

Fig. 2-6. This shows how CF always tries to return the flapping blade to the "normal" position; that is, in a plane 90 degrees to the shaft.

like a restoring spring in this case and we will call it "k" (for restoring function). From Engineering Mechanics we know:

Centrifugal Restoring Moment $= k = I\Omega^2 = \dfrac{1}{3}\ \dfrac{w}{g}\ R^2\Omega^2$

$$\text{(units are in foot-pounds)}$$

where w = blade weight-lbs
     g = accel. gravity-ft/sec
    Ω = rotational speed of rotor-radians/sec
    R = blade radius-ft

From engineering mechanics we also know that the moment of inertia (I) of a free-flapping blade is:

$$I = \dfrac{1}{3}\ \dfrac{w}{g}\ R^2 \quad \text{(units are in foot-pound-sec)}$$

From textbooks on vibration we learn that all things will vibrate when energy is suddenly applied. For example, any particular bell, when struck, always vibrates at the same frequency— its natural frequency, which produces its tone. The bell has very low damping (resistance to vibration) and so it vibrates very readily. A rotor blade vibrates (flaps up and down) about the hub flap axis according to the expression:

$$\omega_n = \sqrt{\dfrac{k}{I}} \quad \text{units are cycles/second}$$

where: ω is small case for Greek letter omega

    ω_2 = natural frequency-cycles per sec
    k = spring restoring moment = ⅓ w / g $R^2\Omega^2$
     = ft-lbs.
    I = moment of intertia flapping blade = ⅓ w / g R^2
     = ft-lb-sec

If we substitute the above values for "k" and "I" into the expression for "ω_n" we get:

$$\omega_n = \sqrt{\dfrac{\dfrac{1}{3}\ \dfrac{w}{g}\ R^2\Omega^2}{\dfrac{1}{3}\ \dfrac{w}{g}\ R^2}}$$

$$\omega_n = \sqrt{\Omega_2}$$

$$\boxed{\omega_n = \Omega}$$

where: ω_n = blade flapping natural frequency
Ω = rotor rotational speed

This simple, yet profound, relationship states that if the rotor blade is unrestrained at its flapping hinge, then *the blade flapping natural frequency is always equal to the rotational speed, no matter what the RPM is!* Yep, it's true!

But where does the 90 degrees phase angle come in? From a study of vibration, a set of curves can be calculated and when plotted look like Fig. 2-7. Let's discuss this set of curves. Figure 2-7 simply says that if you have any vibrating system in which the forcing function is applied at the natural frequency of the system, then the maximum *displacement* will always occur 90 degrees (one quarter of a revolution) *after* the *input force*, regardless of the speed or how much damping is present. What's this damping stuff? Well, to a free-flapping rotor, one kind of damping is the air resistance that opposes flapping. Thus at sea level on a cold day, the air is dense and the air damping is high, whereas at high altitude the rarified air results in relatively poor damping.

Let's pull it all together and see how this set of curves applies to our R/C model rotor. Since a free-flapping rotor always flaps at its natural frequency which is always equal to the rotor RPM, it

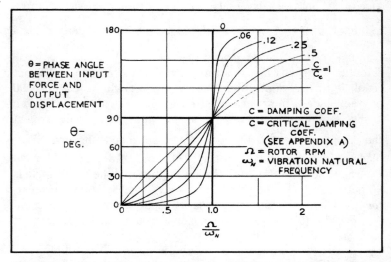

Fig. 2-7. The effect of damping on the phase angle of a blade. For example, if the blade is free flapping (hinged), then the flapping frequency (RPM) is *always* equal to the blade natural flapping frequency, $\frac{\Omega}{W_n}$ =1 and the phase angle is *always* 90 degrees regardless of the damping.

follows that this free-flapping rotor always operates at the point $\frac{\Omega}{\omega_n}$ = 1 in Fig. 2-7. Thus, the phase angle (θ) is always 90 degrees. Now refer back to Fig. 2-4. The blade feels a *lift* force at $\psi = 90$ degrees because of the rotational speed plus the advancing velocity. Likewise it feels a *down* force at $\psi = 270$ degrees, because here the local net velocity is the rotational speed minus the advancing velocity. The result is that because the phase angle is 90 degrees, the maximum displacement is up at $\psi = 180$ degrees and down at $\psi = 180$ degrees and down at $\psi = 360/0$ degrees. Therefore, the blade tends to flap "away" from the onrushing air.

The same phenomenon occurs when the cyclic pitch is applied. Let's go back to Fig. 2-2 for a test. Let's say we apply a cyclic input such that the blade pitch angle is high at $\psi = 180$ degrees and low at $\psi = 360/0$ degrees; what will the machine do? If you say "roll or translate to the right," consider yourself an expert on rotor aerodynamics—well, at least a budding expert! An interesting note in passing: With all rigid rotors (no flapping hinge, although the blades do have some deflection), the natural frequency is always higher than the rotating frequency (the RPM). Thus, this ratio $\frac{\Omega}{\omega_n}$ takes on a value less than unity. All rigid rotors, therefore, operate to the left of $\frac{\Omega}{\omega_n} = 1$ in Fig. 2-7, how *far* to the left of unity being a function of the relative magnitudes of the RPM and the blade retention stiffness which determines the natural frequency. The net result is that all rigid rotors have a phase angle of less than 90 degrees. Indeed this phase angle for any given rigid rotor will even change somewhat from day to day as the atmospheric changes effect the damping ratio $\frac{c}{c_c}$. My scratchbuilt Lockheed Cheyenne four-blade rigid rotor had a phase angle of about 68 degrees. If a rigid rotor is built and installed on the assumption that the phase angle is 90 degrees, the cyclic controls will have what is known as *cross-coupling*. For example, if a nose-up input is applied to a counterclockwise turning rotor, the response would be nose-up and a left roll. More about this later.

Back to the unrestrained flapping rotor in forward flight for a moment. There is an extension of the concept we have been discussing that will suddenly answer some of your questions on rotor behavior. Referring to Fig. 2-3, we found that when the hovering rotor, with no cyclic pitch change was subjected to a translational speed, the advancing blade ($\psi = 90$) exierienced a higher velocity and hence a greater lift force, but the displacement occurred 90 degrees later at $\psi = 180$ degrees. That is, the rotor tended to tilt back as in Fig. 2-3B. (Remember, the incidence on these blades is fixed.)

Now, let's redraw this with a slight variation as shown in Fig. 2-8. Sketch A is a hovering rotor with *forward cyclic pitch* applied to just overcome the backward tilt caused by the translating airflow as we saw earlier. Now here comes a "biggie." Let's redraw the same rotor in B with no change in the position of cyclic pitch, the only change being the *angle* at which the air approaches the same rotor. What happens? The rotor tilts back even more! (Ring any bells with you guys who have suddenly chopped power in level flight at high speed—especially with a rigid rotor—and noticed the model pitch nose-up?) The reason? When you chop power the model immediately begins a descent, i.e., the inflow toward the rotor suddenly resembles B. The advancing blade experiences a higher angle of attack (increased lift *force*) and thus an up displacement occurs in the forward position (phase angle again). The result is that the rotor tilts back and the model pitches nose-up, just as you would expect! Incidentally, the rotor pitches nose-up with a free-teetering rotor, just as it does with the rigid rotor. Why aren't you aware of it? Well, the teetering rotor has less *control power* and even though the rotor pitches, the fuselage continues to dangle due to gravity. You are not so conscious of it, that's all.

This portion of the chapter has been kept short to spotlight the above phenomenon which is the single most important concept leading to the study of stability (discussed in a subsequent chapter).

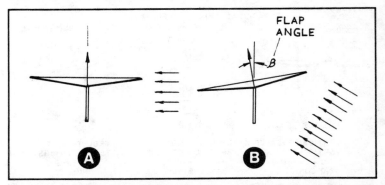

Fig. 2-8. In this figure, notice how a change in an angle of attack makes the rotor flap back. This is the basis for negative angle of attack stability.

If you thoroughly grasp the ideas in the preceding pages, you will have come a long way toward understanding rotor dynamics and aerodynamics.

CORIOLIS

What is it? Why are we going to discuss it here? In a technical sense, I suppose we could say coriolis is "conservation of angular momentum." We see it in effect when a whirling ice skater, with arms outstretched, suddenly raises her arms straight up overhead. You know what happens—her rotational speed suddenly increases. Momentum is essentially mass (or weight) times velocity. The skaters horizontally outstretched arms have a certain amount of momentum as she spins. Because momentum tends to resist change, her rotation speeds up as she raises her arms, because her arms, having a high velocity, tend to maintain that same tangential velocity. Because the radius is now small (arms raised overhead), the rotation rate must increase to satisfy the momentum energy that is present.

What does all this have to do with rotor blades? Every time a rotor blade flaps, coriolis force acts on it. Notice I said *flaps*. Let's review, for a moment. Figure 2-9A is a hovering rotor in which there is *coning* but no *flapping*. Figure 2-9B is a rotor in which cyclic pitch has been applied to tilt the lift vector to provide a horizontal thrust component for transitional flight. In this configuration the blades have coning and they also flap. Hence, these blades do have coriolis forces acting on them. Figure 2-9C is a translating rotor in which the rotating axis is fully gimballed such that the rotational axis and the thrust axis are always coincident. There cannot be any

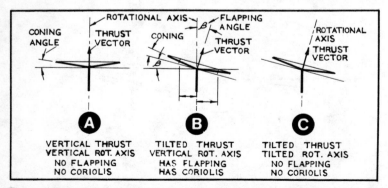

Fig. 2-9. The relationship between coning, flapping, and coriolis (see text for coriolis). When the blades do not flap, there can be no coriolis.

flapping (and consequently no coriolis forces) with this configuration. A good example of this last configuration was the classic Hiller "Rotomatic" system on the full-size machines.

Let's see how coriolis works on a flapping blade. Consider Fig. 2-9B again. The center of gravity of the high blade is closer to the rotational axis than the CG of the low blade. Once each revolution, therefore, each flapping blade moves nearer to the axis and therefore experiences an in-plane *acceleration* as it flaps up. Likewise, when it flaps to a lower angle, the CG moves away from the axis and the blade feels an in-plane *deceleration*. Obviously this situation creates an in-plane vibration in the rotor.

To give you some idea of the seriousness of the effects of coriolis, very large, heavy, multi-blade helicopters have built-in "lead-lag" hinges to prevent the in-plane forces from being transmitted into the hub. Without these hinges (and their snubbing dampers), the structural loads in the hub and the vibrations in the entire airframe would be intolerable. The lead-lag hinges, therefore, are quite necessary and do a fine job on the large machines.

Relatively small helicopters with two blade teetering rotors (such as the Hiller H-23 series or the Bell machines) can do without lead-lag hinges by building the teetering hub strong, so that when one blade is trying to accelerate in-plane, the moment is carried across the hub and absorbed by the opposite blade which is simultaneously trying to decelerate.

Chapter 3

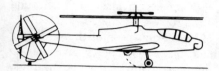

Performance

In the case of full-size helicopters, *performance* encompasses many factors such as maximum speed, rate of climb, service ceiling, maximum payload, etc. With the R/C model counterpart, however, performance entails essentially two questions: Does the model have enough power to fly?* And, why does it act so strangely in certain flight conditions? This second condition, as discussed here, has to do with model response to changing power requirements as a function of horizontal or vertical speed and is not, as such, a function of stability. Stability is discussed in a subsequent chapter.

POWER REQUIRED

There are several distinct physical functions, each of which requires that power be expended in order that any helicopter be capable of performing even the simplest maneuver such as hover or level forward flight. For any given flight condition these individual power requirements are directly additive, and when plotted as *total power required* versus speed, they present a rather curiously shaped curve. The shape of this curve is the basis for understanding the answer to the second of the two questions above. Let's look at what makes up this total power required.

INDUCED POWER

You will recall in Chapter 1, it was stated that as a rotor turns

---

*See Appendix B

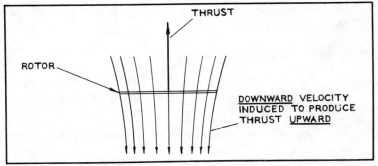

Fig. 3-1. The shape of the air inflow of a hovering rotor.

and produces lift, two kinds of drag must be overcome. One of these is induced drag, which is an inherent and inseparable result of producing lift. In Fig. 3-1 we have a lifting rotor (i.e., thrusting upward). For the rotor to thrust *upward,* it must impart *downward* momentum to a large mass of air as indicated by the arrows beneath the rotor. Simply put, Newton's Third Law essentially states that for every force there is an equal and opposite force. Now then, it is obvious that power must be expended to accelerate this large mass of air to a high downward velocity (momentum equals mass times velocity). It is equally obvious that the power required to do this is proportional to the downward velocity of this air mass. The power needed to accelerate this air mass is called *induced power.* Actually, thrust upward is a function of the square of the downward air velocity (commonly referred to as "downwash" or "induced velocity.") The power to produce this thrust is called induced power, and it is proportional to the cube of the induced velocity!

Here then is a "biggie." If we have a very large area (large diameter rotor) we can produce high thrust by accelerating this large mass of air to only a moderate velocity, whereas if we have a small area (jet tail pipe for example) the same mass of air *per unit of time* requires a tremendously high induced velocity, and therefore, the induced power expenditure is exceedingly high. Now we see why the helicopter rotor is the most efficient heavier-than-air vertical lifting device. Since in hover, induced power (P_i) comprises about 60% of total power required, it behooves us to select a design where V_i is low because induced power, as stated earlier, is a function of the cube of the induced velocity (V_i)!

Let's carry the above concept of induced velocity a little further. Remember that lift is produced by imparting an increased velocity (acceleration) to a given mass of air, or stated mathematically it would read:

Thrust = (M) (ΔV_i)   where M = air mass
ΔV_i = (reads "delta Vee")
= the increase in air velocity through the rotor, or *induced velocity.*

Now then, what would happen if we, using cyclic pitch, tilted the rotor slightly as shown in Fig. 3-2? The vertical lift is still essentially the same, but now a horizontal thrust vector is introduced to cause the rotor to translate at some horizontal speed. The result is that now a much larger mass of air *per unit of time* flows through the rotor. Referring back to the equation $T = (M)(\Delta V_i)$ to maintain the same thrust, (ΔV_i) can now be much smaller because we have just seen that, in forward flight, M becomes very large. Because (ΔV_i) is reduced in forward flight, the induced power to produce a given thrust decreases with increasing translational speed. For a typical rotor, *induced power* when plotted as a function of speed would look like Fig. 3-3.

Notice the left-hand side of the curve near the hover condition: the curve divides. The upper line (solid) is the induced power required out-of-ground effect (OGE), that is, when hovering with the rotor disc higher than about one and a half rotor diameters above the surface. Strangely enough, the induced power required remains essentially constant from this point up to any height we are likely to hover the R/C model.

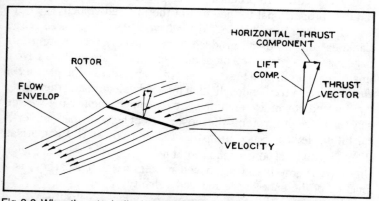

Fig. 3-2. When the rotor is tilted by cyclic pitch, the horizontal component of thrust moves (translates) the rotor and the new inflow pattern can be seen.

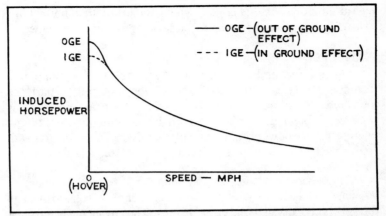

Fig. 3-3. This curve shows the relationship between speed and power required to produce lift. Notice that a rotor hovering near the ground (approx. one dia.) requires less power than one hovering higher.

The lower line (dashed) represents the induced power required to hover *in-ground-effect* (IGE), ie., with the landing gear just clear of the ground. Notice that IGE requires appreciably less power. This phenomenon is explained by the "experts" with a couple of different theories: (1) The downwash forms a relatively high-pressure cushion between the rotor and the ground which reduces the induced velocity, thus reducing the induced power. (2) The downwash impinges the ground, is deflected radially outward, up, and returns back down through the rotor again—this time with a higher initial velocity, thus requiring *less increase in the induced velocity* and consequently less induced power. Figure 3-4 shows what this recirculatory flow pattern looks like. Take your pick. I *do* know that the second condition *does* occur, at least to some degree, because during many IGE hover performance tests of full-size machines, I have observed a sudden rise in outside air temperature

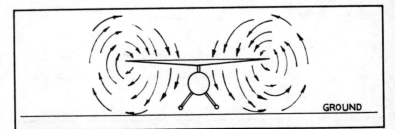

Fig. 3-4. The recirculation of air when hovering in ground effect (IGE).

37

measured from the helicopter which indicated that hot engine exhaust gases were recirculating, at least as part of the downwash.

PROFILE POWER

Again referring back to Chapter 1, the term *profile power* was introduced. We said that it is the power required to part the molecules of air and to overcome skin friction as the blade is dragged through the air in the zero lift condition. Interestingly enough, profile power required is relatively constant with airspeed, from hover throughout the speed range our R/C models are likely to fly.

The obvious question is: Why should it be essentially constant as a function of speed? Well, the profile power of an isolated blade is directly proportional to the speed it sees. The advancing blade does require more profile power with increasing speed, but the retreating blade is requiring less profile power with increasing forward speed due to the reduced local velocity (Ω R-V) on the retreating blade. Profile power required as a function of speed is in Fig. 3-5.

PARASITE POWER

Parasite power is the term given to another factor required in determining the total power required. It includes the expenditure needed to drag the helicopter fuselage, landing gear, horizontal or vertical tail stabilizers, scoops, rotor hub, antenna, switch handles, and all the other hundred and one protuberances exposed to the air slipstream. (Tail rotor power developed in producing thrust is

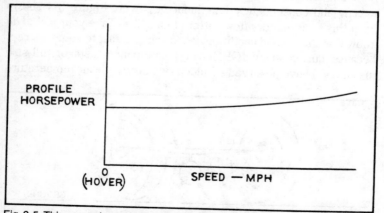

Fig. 3-5. This curve shows the relation between speed and power required just to rotate the rotor (not accounting for lift).

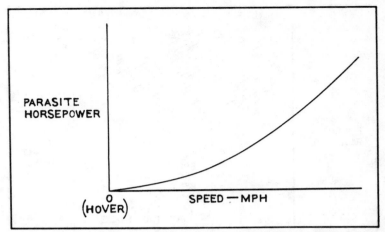

Fig. 3-6. This curve shows the relation between speed and power required to drag the fuselage, landing gear, door handles, etc. through the air. Notice it is zero in hover, which is what you would expect.

listed separately). Parasite power is, of course, zero in hover because the horizontal airflow is zero, but it increases as the *cube* of the airspeed! For example, if the airspeed doubles, the parasite drag becomes eight times as great. The curve of parasite drag therefore looks something like Fig. 3-6.

OTHER FACTORS

Miscellaneous items contributing to the overall power required, but to a lesser degree, include tail rotor induced and profile power, which for our purposes can be considered ten percent of the main rotor induced and profile power. This is a fairly accurate "rule of thumb" for hover, but is less accurate in forward flight. Other items include mechanical friction in bearings, gears, belts, and power absorbed by a cooling fan. Realistic loss factors for these items, obtained from Machine Design handbooks, are presented in Appendix B. For our purposes, these miscellaneous items can be considered to be independent of airspeed.

When the values of the main rotor *induced, profile,* and the airframe *parasite* power required at each airspeed are added, the *total power required* presents a rather curiously shaped curve as shown in Fig. 3-7. The straight line across the top is conventionally plotted as the engine rated horsepower minus all the miscellaneous items. In other words, it is the net horsepower available to fly the machine.

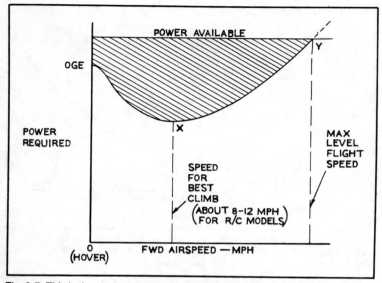

Fig. 3-7. This is the total added power required from Figs. 3-3, 3-5, and 3-6. The shaded portion would be excess power available for climb. The fastest climb would be at X (about 10-12 mph most models). Y represents the maximum level flight forward speed.

POWER REQUIRED AND ROTOR RESPONSE

Let's chew on Fig. 3-7 a bit, and I think we will begin to see some of the answers to the second question in the introduction to this section. First, the shaded portion between the power required and power available represents excess power that can be converted into climb at a given speed. Figure 3-7 indicates something very strange—namely, if we have two identical helicopters at, say, fifty feet above the ground on a calm day, and one is hovering while the other one is flying level at speed "x" (in Fig. 3-7) which is about 8-12 mph for R/C models, then the machine flying at speed "x" requires less power than the one that is hovering! Yep, it's true.

Now we can see why: (a) a model that doesn't have enough power to hover on a calm day will hover with ease in a wind; (b) a model hovering in a wind begins to settle if it is slowly backed away from the wind; (c) a model hovering IGE, on a calm day, begins to settle slightly (moves off ground cushion) and then rapidly climbs when forward cyclic control is applied (no change in power or collective position). In this last case, as the machine moves from hover out to speed x with no change in power, the excess power is converted into climb. Other "goodies" to be gleamed from Fig. 3-7 are that a model has the fastest rate of climb at speed x, and also has the slowest sink rate in pure autorotation at speed x. The R/C helicopter modeler would do well to study the curve of Fig. 3-7 (the curves of no two helicopters are identical but they do all have the same general shape) to visualize what part of the curve his model is on when flying. It will help him anticipate what is likely to happen next.

POWER SETTLING

One other flight characteristic is worthy of discussion because it frequently occurs. When it does occur, the one on the transmitter should understand what is happening and what to do about it. Incidentally, it has little or nothing to do with the curve of Fig. 3-7.

The flight attitude involves vertical descent. Let's review a hovering rotor in calm air as shown in Fig. 3-8. In case A the air enters the rotor from the top, of course, and is accelerated (down) to the induced velocity required to produce hover. Now then, if the power to this hovering rotor is reduced, the helicopter will begin to descend vertically. When the descent rate has increased, and is equal to the *mean induced velocity,* the rotor enters what is known as the *vortex ring state* to the aerodynamist or *power settling* to you or me. It is a strange phenomenon and the one on the transmitter can be lulled into it without any warning. The ironical part of the power settling is that if power is increased, the machine *continues* its vertical descent! In fact, the more power that is applied to the rotor

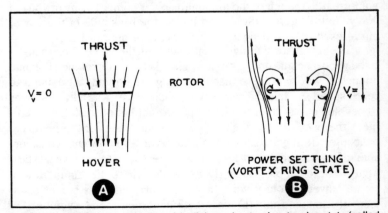

Fig. 3-8. A graphic representation of the little-understood vortex ring state (called power settling). A shows air flow in a normal hover. B shows the model descending while generating lift. The descent is due to the recirculation of air through the rotor.

to check the descent rate, the faster the vortices in Fig. 3-8B recirculate out, and up, and back down through the rotor, this time at higher induced velocity.

Although it is true that the rotor is producing more and more thrust and is therefore climbing, it is climbing in a vertically moving air column that is descending faster than the machine is climbing! The net result is that the machine continues to sink even with full power. To put it plainly, it is kinda like trying to swim up a waterfall.

Well, what can we do about it, other than avoid it? Fortunately there is a simple recovery procedure, should you find yourself in this condition. Simply apply cyclic pitch (nose-down is natural) and the machine will immediately slip out of the vortex ring state into undisturbed air and will immediately respond to power application. The writer has seen several R/C models and one full-size machine go clear into the ground (literally). The modelers claimed servo failure because they didn't understand what was happening, but the men in the full-size machine should have known better.

POWER REQUIRED: ROTARY WING VS FIXED WING

And last, for this performance section, I can't resist the comparison between helicopters and airplanes. Figure 3-9 reveals some interesting points. Does anything strike you as significant about these two curves? From the minimum power point to the higher speeds, they are of similar shape, aren't they? (The speeds, of course, will vary.) Indeed, the curves even follow the same trend somewhat to the left of the minimum power point. To any of you old Navy "tail daggers," the dotted line is the back side of the power curve used by WWII fighters during carrier approaches.

The interesting thing is that man first flew a heavier-than-air fixed wing machine only after an engine had been developed that had enough power to pull the machine along the ground fast enough to reach speed x. Thus the rotary wing counterpart was a little slower to develop due to the need for a lightweight but powerful engine to meet the needs of the higher power requirement of the hovering helicopter. It might surprise you, however, to know that considerable effort was being put forth in the late 1800s to achieve vertical flight. For example, as early as 1877 Enrico Fortanini flew a steam-powered rotary wing (non-man-carrying) to a height of 40 feet and remained aloft 20 seconds. Furthermore, on November 13, 1907 Paul Cornu lifted himself to five feet altitude (tethered) and remained aloft for about one minute. He used tandem rotors, each one 24 feet in diameter, and a 24-horsepower Antoinette engine.

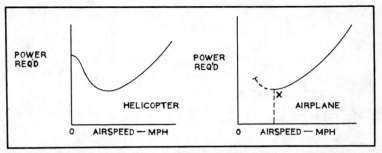

Fig. 3-9. Comparison between power required of a rotary wing (left) and a fixed wing (right).

Also in 1909, Berliner produced a two-engine, counter-rotating rotor machine that lifted a pilot untethered. Thus, just as at Kitty Hawk six years earlier with the Wright Brothers and their fixed-wing machine, the age of helicopters arrived.

Chapter 4

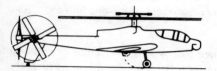

Stability

How can something be explained when it doesn't exist? I'm being facetious, of course. Helicopters do have stability (poor, but nevertheless stability)—in fact, several kinds. It is the unfortunate combination of forces and moments resulting from the interaction of speed stability, angle of attack stability, and rotor damping that create the problem. Hovering a helicopter has been likened to trying to balance oneself on a beach ball. "It seems like no matter what you do it's wrong, and if you don't do anything that's even worse!"

Before we get into the subject, let's review several terms and a short definition of each:

Trim—an aircraft is *trimmed* in steady flight when the resultant forces and moments are equal to zero. To a modeler, this is meaningful primarily in the hover condition. That is, it is more comfortable to hover a model with the trim levers adjusted in pitch, roll, and yaw, so as to eliminate the necessity of steady forces on the primary levers.

Stability—concerns the behavior of a model after it has been disturbed slightly from the trimmed equilibrium condition. There are two kinds of stability, and each of these may be positive, negative or neutral.

Static stability—a model has positive static stability if there is an *initial* tendency for it to return to its trimmed condition after a disturbance, such as stick pulse or a gust. The model has negative stability if it tends to diverge, or it has neutral stability if it tends to remain in the attitude to which it is disturbed.

Dynamic stability—this concerns the oscillation of an R/C helicopter about its trim position following a disturbance from trim. If the oscillation increases in amplitude, the model has negative dynamic stability. If the amplitude diminishes, the model has positive dynamic stability, or if the oscillation continues without change in amplitude, the dynamic stability is said to be neutral.

Following rate—the following rate is the equilibrium rate of pitch or roll of a model per unit input at the *swashplate*.

Control sensitivity—control sensitivity is the equilibrium rate of pitch or roll or a model per unit input at the *pilot's control*.

Damping in pitch (or roll)—the magnitude of the moment due to the relative tilting velocity between the rotor disc and the fuselage is a measure of damping in pitch or roll. This moment is a function of rotor tilting rate, fuselage rotational inertia, rotor RPM, and airloads on the fuselage. Thus, small, lightweight models having low mass (or weight) and/or high RPM teetering rotors will likely have low damping in pitch or roll. Teetering rotors, however, with some form of stabilization such as a stabilizer bar or a control rotor have appreciably better damping in pitch or roll. In the special case of the rigid rotor, the pitch or roll moment generated by the rotor is directly transmitted into the airframe, and so the *relative* velocities are essentially nil. (The special case of the rigid rotor is further discussed in Chapter 5.)

Let's look at some of the above characteristics in more detail in the context of how they affect the behavior of an R/C model.

Speed stability—in Chapter 2 a hovering rotor was discussed in which the controls were fixed and to which a translational velocity was added. Remember the result when horizontal speed was added? The rotor flapped "back" or away from the oncoming horizontal flow. Figure 4-1 is a similar lifting rotor that is advancing, or translating, and to which, in A, a forward cyclic pitch input has tilted the rotor forward so that the thrust vector is coincident with the shaft and there is, of course, no flapping. Now then, in B, the horizontal velocity has been *increased* but the rotor cyclic pitch input remains as it was in A. What happens? The rotor again flaps "back" just as it did in Chapter 2 going from hover to a given speed. The result is that the tip-path-plane tilts back with increased speed, the thrust vector now having two components, one lifting vertically and the other in a horizontal force which tends to *slow* the helicopter *horizontal speed*. When the helicopter has decelerated to the original

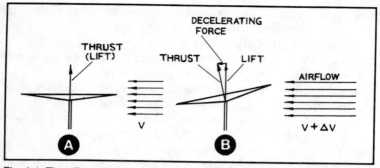

Fig. 4-1. The effect of horizontal air flow on a hovering rotor. This subject was briefly covered in Chapter 2; here we are talking about the stability aspect.

speed of A, the rotor tip-path-plane also returns to the original stabilized position of A. Conversely, if the speed in A were suddenly decreased, the rotor tip-path-plane would tilt forward, producing an accelerating component of forward thrust and thus restoring the rotor to the original translational speed of A. This, then, by the definition of static stability, says that *all rotors have inherent positive speed stability*.

Angle of attack stability—for this, we go back to Chapter 2 with particular emphasis on Fig. 2-8 and the discussion centered thereon. There we saw that a rotor in translation, i.e., horizontal velocity, with cyclic input to maintain a vertical thrust vector, tilts back if the angle of attack increased. Let's redraw it as Fig. 4-2. Now conditions A and B of Fig. 4-2 are the same as those in Fig. 4-1 A and B, but notice that, because of the aft tilt of the rotor when the translation speed is increased in B, the angle of attack in C is even larger, as discussed in Chapter 2. Once this angle of attack begins to increase, it continues to increase until the horizontal offsetting speed component of the lift vector becomes so large that the machine undershoots the initial trim speed. Therefore, by definition again, *all rotors have inherent negative angle of attack stability*.

Whereas speed stability is symmetrical about the trim point (that is, restoring moments are equal in effectiveness whether the model is returning from a below-trim speed or an above-trim speed condition), angle of attack stability is not symmetrical. Because the rotor is lifting, angle of attack stability is more sensitive in the nose-up condition as indicated in Fig. 4-3.

A close look at the curve shows that for each unit of nose-up angle, the rotor nose-up moment response is much greater than the nose-down moment response to the same unit increment of nose-

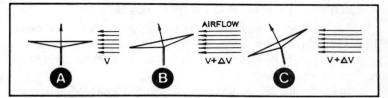

Fig. 4-2. The hovering rotor, showing that the higher the translation speed, the more the rotor flaps back. This introduces speed and angle of attack stability.

down angle. This coupling of unsymmetrical pitching moment with angle of attack also constitutes a measure of stability, or in this case, instability. Because of this unique interdependent combination of positive speed stability, negative angle of attack stability, and rotor flapwise damping, basically *all rotors* are statically and dynamically unstable. The behavior of the whole model, therefore, is to a great extent, dependent on the *relative magnitudes* of the above rotor characteristics in concert as established by the particular rotor configuration. We will consider four fundamental rotor configurations: (1) two-bladed teetering rotors; (2) two-bladed teetering rotor with some means of stabilization augmentation such as a control rotor; (3) a three- (or more) bladed rigid rotor without; and (4) with a closed-loop-feedback stabilizing gyro (that is, a gyro having 100% authority over the rotor).

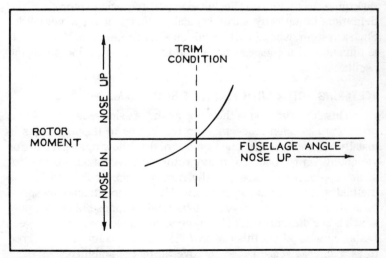

Fig. 4-3. This graph "says" that with a lifting rotor, the more the nose is raised, the greater the flap back. A nose-down attitude produces much less nose-down rotor flap.

STABILITY OF THE TEETERING ROTOR IN HOVER

Figure 4-4 is a conventional two-bladed teetering rotor model in hover. The letters (a) throught (g) represent time sequences covering one complete cycle of what is referred to as the *short period oscillation* experienced in hover.

In (a) the model has just been influenced by a stick pulse or a gust which tilts the rotor to the right. Because there is now a horizontal component of thrust, the model begins to translate to the right. We know that the rotor has positive speed stability and thus it flaps back at position (b), creating a counterclockwise rolling moment about the model CG. Due to very low flapwise damping with this rotor configuration, the rotor continues to flap back to the left with the counterclockwise roll until the translation velocity is zero and the model is now tilted to the left at position (c). Lateral translation again takes place as before, except now to the left, and the rotor again begins to respond to positive speed stability as it passes the center at (d). A comparision of (d) to (a) shows that in both cases the model is tilted, but in (d) it is translating whereas in (a) its velocity was zero. The above half cycle is again repeated, and at position (g) the tilt will be steeper and the velocity higher.

Thus, following a disturbance from hover, the low damped teetering rotor does not initially tend to return to trim, and furthermore, when it finally does begin to return, it overshoots trim in ever diverging oscillations. The low-damped teetering rotor then, by definition, is statically and dynamically unstable in the hover mode. Such a system, whether with a full-size helicopter or an R/C model, is difficult and unpleasant to fly due to the short period diverging oscillations.

TEETERING ROTOR WITH FLAPWISE BLADE DAMPING

This configuration is the same as the previous one except that provision has been made to snub the blades in flapping. This is usually accomplished by one or more of the following: a gyro bar or weighted control paddles, heavy rotor tip weights and/or hub-to-shaft flapping restriction (usually rubber or springs). All of these methods have one thing in common. They are not affected by speed or angle of attack stability, and thus tend to oppose blade flapping which is the direct result of both speed and angle of attack changes. Let's see what effect this reduced flapping characteristic (referred to as a *damped rotor* has on the overall model stability.

Referring to Fig. 4-5, we have a teetering, highly damped rotor that, as before, has just been upset by a gust of stick pulse. The

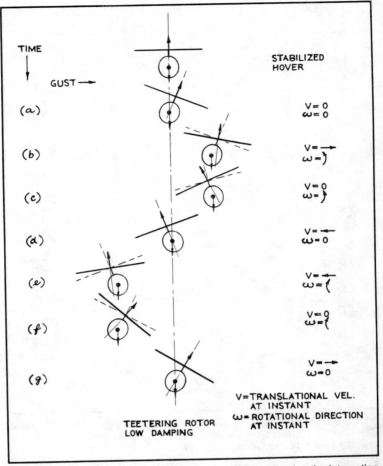

Fig. 4-4. This is a time sequence beginning at the top showing the interacting between speed and angle of attack stability with the swinging air frame (low damped rotor). This is the so-called short-period oscillation encountered in most all helicopters (to some degree or another).

machine again moves to the right because of the horizontal component of the thrust vector to position (b). Now at (c) the fuselage has overtaken the rotor tilt (due to high rotor damping) and thus the thrust vector is again essentially through the CG of the model. Actually, steps (b) and (c) are occurring simultaneously, but are shown separately for clarification. At positions (d) and (e), the same process is occurring as at (b) and (c) and the machine is slowly decelerating the lateral translation, and is slowly rolling coun-

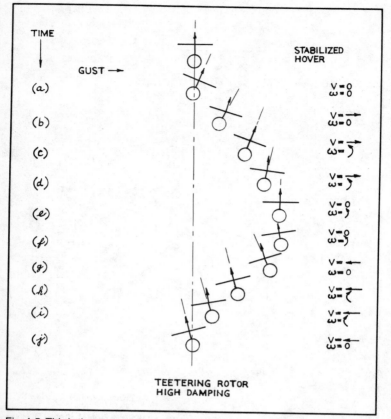

Fig. 4-5. This is the same as Fig. 4-4 except it shows the effect of added flapwise rotor damping on the period of oscillation (time for one cycle). The longer the time, the easier the machine is to control.

terclockwise. At position (f) the velocity is again almost zero but the fuselage continues to overshoot, causing the machine to roll to the left; for probably a brief instant after (f), the translation *and* angular velocity are both near zero although the model is tilted to the left. Thus the process repeats itself over and over, oscillating back and forth, (or, as in our example, laterally). This rotor configuration then also has negative static and dynamic stability. The big difference is that when rotor damping is added or increased, the oscillation period (the time to complete one instability cycle described above) becomes longer and the divergence, while still present, occurs slower. This permits the person on the transmitter a much longer time to "update" the position and attitude of his model with smaller corrective inputs (or even to anticipate inputs). The bottom line is that *increased rotor damping slows the rotor response*, which is undesirable from the standpoint of controllability, but *decreases* the *instability* which is desirable from the standpoint of flying pleasure.

STABILITY OF THE RIGID ROTOR

Although the rigid rotor retains the same inherent characteristics of positive speed and negative angle of attack stability, the fact that the blades are not free to flap (they *do* deflect) imposes very high rotor damping. The new result, without going through another time study of a hover oscillation, is that this configuration has the longest period of oscillation and the slowest rate of divergence of all the rotor configurations to date and is, therefore, the *least unstable* of all. It should be noted, however, that in Chapter 2 (Fig. 2-8) we saw that the rigid rotor "appeared" to be more susceptible to angle-of-attack instability than the flapping blade rotor. The reason for the misconception is that the low damped teetering rotor has less control power, and through the teetering rotor pitches up even *more*, the fuselage of the model continues to dangle due to gravity. So the man on the transmitter is not as aware that the teetering rotor pitches more than the rigid rotor.

RIGID ROTOR WITH 100% CLOSED LOAD STABILITY FEEDBACK

This configuration is the same as the previous one except that the rotor has a free-gimballed gyro, mounted above or below it, so that the gyro has one hundred percent authority over the main rotor (Fig. 4-6). Although this configuration is still somewhat beyond the

Fig. 4-6. A four-blade rigid rotor with the rate gyro which has 100% authority over the blades.

current R/C helicopter "state of the art" from the standpoint of practical reality, it is worthy of discussion here. It is the only rotor system, to my knowledge, to have positive static and dynamic stability (without "black boxes")! Perhaps this discussion will spark some interest in research into the system with variations on the theme.

The system is unique because the gyro of this hovering model maintains an independent position in space without regard to flight conditions until, and only after, an input is sent to it by the man on the transmitter.

Let's look at this configuration in hover after a gust has tried to uspet it. No time-lapsed figure is necessary here either. As in all systems, the rotor initially responds by beginning to tilt away from the gust, but is considerably restrained by the high damping of the rigid rotor—or another way of saying it, by the inertia of the entire model airframe. Furthermore, the *gyro does not feel the upsetting signal in any way* and therefore remains at a constant position in space. As the rotor begins to respond by tilting in pitch or roll due to the gust, the gyro automatically applies a corrective input to the rotor that is directly proportional to the difference between the angle of the gyro plane and the rotor tip-path-plane. The result is quite astounding! The rotor tip-path-plane returns to its trim position, and the model maintains the smooth solid flight so characteristic of its full-size counterpart rather than bobbing around like a cork on rough water, as so many of our present models do.

STABILITY OF THE TEETERING ROTOR IN FORWARD FLIGHT

The motion of a helicopter model in forward flight after a disturbance from a trimmed condition depends, again, on speed and angle of attack stability, rotor damping, and to some extent on the size and location of a horizontal stabilizer near the tail rotor (sometimes these surfaces are set at a 45 degree angle to serve two functions simultaneously). In the hover stability just concluded, we saw that positive speed stability combined with negative angle of attack stability and low rotor damping resulted in the most difficult configuration to hover. The same trend prevails in forward flight.

Figure 4-7 is a helicopter in forward flight which has encountered a gust that pitches it nose-down. The question is, "will the helicopter recover to level flight at the trim speed again?" Let's take a look at what happens and then summarize the effects of each of the stability characteristics on the overall picture.

In (a) the machine is upset to a nose-down attitude. Since a

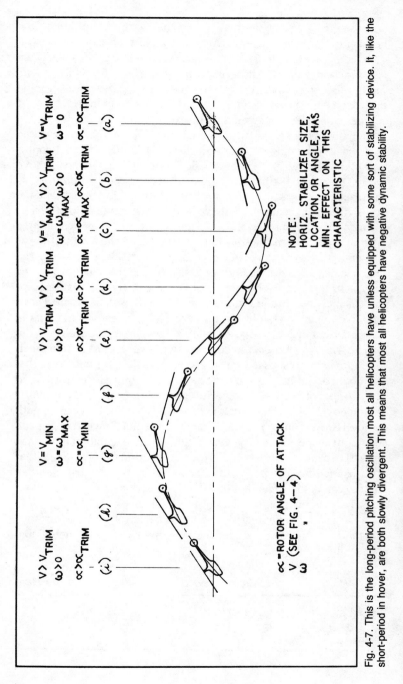

Fig. 4-7. This is the long-period pitching oscillation most all helicopters have unless equipped with some sort of stabilizing device. It, like the short-period in hover, are both slowly divergent. This means that most all helicopters have negative dynamic stability.

53

component of the weight vector is along the flight path, the helicopter increases speed. At position (b), because of the increased speed (above trim), the positive speed stability flaps the rotor back, producing a nose-up moment and nose-up rotation. The increased angle of attack increases even to a greater nose-up angle due to the negative angle of attack stability inherent in all rotors. At (c) the helicopter has leveled off below trim altitude but at a speed higher than trim speed, which consequently, with the rotor tilted back, causes the model to go into a climb. At (d), with the helicopter now climbing, the speed begins to decrease although it is still above trim. The rotor aft-tilt also begins to decrease. At position (e), as the machine passes through trim altitude, the angle of attack and the speed are both greater than they were at position (a). Positions (f) through (h) continue the above process until the model completes one full cycle of oscillation at position (i) which is the trim altitude at the outset. Now, however, the angle of attack is greater, the machine has a greater nose-down attitude, and the speed is greater than at the outset. The bottom line is that the oscillations are increasing in amplitude and the model is said, by definition, to have negative dynamic stability in forward flight. These oscillations in forward flight in general have a much longer period and are given the classic name of *Pheugoid* in contrast to the very short period oscillations in hover discussed earlier. Most modelers are not aware that their helicopter has the above described instability in forward flight for two reasons. First, the period is much longer than the short-period hover oscillation—on the order of 15 to 30 seconds depending on the machine. Most R/C models are not flown straight and level for this period of time very often, so the oscillation never has time to become established. Further, the period is long enough that if the oscillation does begin, the man on the transmitter has plenty of time to correct it, indeed, most of the corrections are made without conscious thought on the part of the modeler.

We can now summarize the three basic rotor characteristics and their overall effect on the R/C helicopter which will determine its stability:

If	Oscillation Period	Airframe Rotation Rate
Speed stability is made less positive	Is increased	Is decreased

If	Oscillation Period	Airframe Rotation Rate
Angle of attack stability made less negative	Is increased	Is decreased
Rotor damping is increased	Is increased	Is decreased

From the above it is obvious that the *least unstable* model will have less positive speed stability, less negative angle of attack stability, and more rotor damping. It all boils down to limiting the rotor from flapping any more than absolutely necessary in order to improve the stability of the model. As we have seen, this can be accomplished in a variety of ways or in combinations thereof, including such things as increased rotor tip weights, reduced rotor RPM, snubbing dampers or springs to limit teetering action, a rigid hub, and/or some form of stabilizing bar (with or without control paddles) to provide a corrective input signal in opposition to excessive flapping. The stabilizer bar or control rotor in its various forms is discussed in Chapter 5.

FORWARD SWEEP TO IMPROVE STABILITY?

I can't resist discussing here one more interesting and unique modification that can be applied to a four-bladed rigid rotor with 100% authority gyro. This modification results in an effective means of offsetting gusts when the machine has translational speed. The result is that the model has even better static stability. Would you believe forward sweep applied to the main rotor blades? It rather goes against some of the things stated in Chapter 1, doesn't it? Actually, Chapter 1 was concerned with rotor blades in general whereas the rigid rotor with a 100% authority gyro is a unique case. Up to about three degrees, maximum, forward sweep can be incorporated in this *(and only this)* configuration. You say, "How in the world can forward sweep improve static stability in gusty air? I don't believe it!" Well, it *does*. In my scratchbuilt model of the rigid rotor Lockheed Cheyenne bravery ceased at about two degrees forward sweep on each of the four blades, but the improvement was quite noticeable when the forward sweep was later incorporated. I would like to complete this section on stability with an exercise showing how this works.

Figure 4-8 is the top view of a four-bladed rigid rotor with a rate gyro having 100% authority over the blades (except for the blade feedback due to forward sweep being discussed here). Each blade has mass balance weights on the tip to maintain the blade chordwise center of gravity forward of the center of pressure. The blades are rigidly mounted except, of course, in feathering, and are swept forward such that both the center of gravity and center of pressure are ahead of the feathering axis. We have all the "tools" in Chapters 1 and 2 with which to follow the concept. Consider that the rotor is translating toward the top of the page and that it has just encountered a gust which is tending to upset the rotor nose-up. Now then, we know the blade cannot flap, being rigidly attached, but it can and does, nevertheless, tend to *deflect* upward at $\psi = 180$ degrees (forward). Because both the CG and CP are ahead of the feathering axis, the blade (A) as it tends to deflect up (out of the paper) at $\psi = 180$ degrees, will actually try to rotate nose-up about the feather axis (due to forward sweep). The gyro which controls the blade feathering, however, prevents any blade feathering, and so the gyro arm connected to blade (A) pitch arm feels an up force (out of the paper). The up force on blade (A) is the same as a down force on the gyro arm of blade (C). The gyro, being free to process, does so with a down (into the paper) displacement 90 degrees later when the blade (C) is at $\psi = 90$ degrees as shown in Fig. 4-9.

Blade (C) having received a nose-down feathering input from the gyro at $\psi = 90$ degrees, develops the maximum down (into the

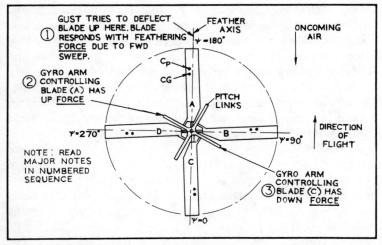

Fig. 4-8. Rigid rotor gust control using forward sweep; see Fig. 4-9.

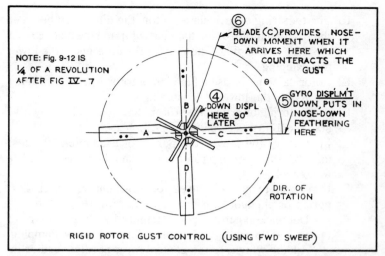

NOTE: Fig. 9-12 IS ¼ OF A REVOLUTION AFTER FIG IV-7

⑥ BLADE (C) PROVIDES NOSE-DOWN MOMENT WHEN IT ARRIVES HERE WHICH COUNTERACTS THE GUST

④ DOWN DISPL HERE 90° LATER

⑤ GYRO DISPLM'T DOWN, PUTS IN NOSE-DOWN FEATHERING HERE

DIR. OF ROTATION

RIGID ROTOR GUST CONTROL (USING FWD SWEEP)

Fig. 4-9. This is similar to Fig. 4-8 except the rotor has rotated 90 degrees. These figures are a study in the dynamic stability of a rigid rotor with a gyro having 100 percent authority over the main rotor. It is the only system, to date, (without electric black boxes, etc.) to have positive dynamic stability in forward flight. The figures are studied by reading the notes in their numbered sequence.

paper) deflection (and thus a moment) at ψ = approximately 160 degrees which automatically corrects for the nose-up moment created by the gust just one half a rotor revolution earlier! The correction is automatic and is applied so fast that the gust is scarcely noticed. The reader has probably noted that for the correction to be perfect, it would have come out at ψ = 180 degrees instead of ψ = 160 degrees. The 160 degree position is of course due to the fact that the phase angle of a restrained blade as applied earlier is less than 90 degrees—on my Cheyenne it was about 68 degrees. The very slight left roll during the gust correction is not noticeable. (Nor was it on the full-size Cheyenne.)

One last caution: *Do not try this forward sweep on free-flapping rotors* which are not controlled by a 100% authority gyro. Forward sweep on any configuration other than that just discussed can and likely will be dangerous in the form of a divergent dynamic blade instability which could destroy the rotor.

A brief summary of stability is in order because of the importance and also due to the complexity of the subject:

☐ All rotors inherently have positive speed stability.
☐ All rotors inherently have negative angle-of-attack stability.

- In a teetering or articulated rotor, the difference between the rotational rate of the flapping rotor and the fuselage is a measure of damping. The greater the difference, the lower the damping.
- Rotor damping is also a function of rotor RPM. The higher the RPM, the lower the damping.
- All teetering or articulated rotors have neutral or negative static stability (assuming no SAS).
- In general, the longer the period of oscillation, the less unstable the teetering rotor will be and the easier it will be to control.
- In general, to increase the period of oscillation (either short period or pheugoid) change the following:
  - Decrease positive speed stability by slaving the rotor to a gyro or control rotor. This improves damping. Adding weight to the control rotor paddles further increases damping, but reduces the following rate making control response more sluggish. Increasing paddle areas will offset the effect of increased paddle weight making the response more crisp.
  - Increase the blade tip mass-balance weight as discussed but remember the centrifugal force on the weights. They can cause very high stresses.
  - Snub the flapping or teetering hinge action by rubber or spring dampers.
- A three or four blade rigid rotor with a rate gyro having 100% authority and with forward sweep in the blades has positive static and dynamic stability.

Chapter 5

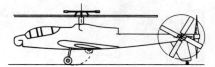

Controllability

In the previous chapter we discussed the behavior of a rotor as a result of an external stimulus such as a gust. In this chapter we will look at the response of a rotor to control input. Several variables are involved, some of which we have already discovered including the period of an oscillation if dynamically unstable, following rate, and control sensitivity. To the above we can add one more, *control power*, which is defined here as "the ability of a rotor to generate a moment about the model CG per unit of control input" (Figs. 5-1, 5-2).

Optimum values for some of the above variables are known. For example, we found in Chapter 4 that the longer the period, i.e., the time to complete one cycle of oscillation due to dynamic instability, the easier the helicopter is to control. Also, high control power is desirable as this broadens the CG range, or to put it another way, the CG position is not nearly as critical as with a low control power model. The other two characteristics (rotor following rate and control sensitivity), however, are not so easy to optimize. (By *optimize*, we mean determine the values that the man on the transmitter is most comfortable with in controlling the model). For instance, the optimum rotor following rate is related to the dynamic stability. The more unstable the rotor, the more critical the limits of the rotor following rate. Conversely, a highly stable rotor is easy to control throughout a very broad range of following rates once the modeler has familiarized himself with the particular configuration.

Fig. 5-1. A contest flight. The man in the dark hat is controlling the model by levers on his hand held radio transmitter. The other man is a judge evaluating the modelers skill.

Control sensitivity is largely a matter of personal opinion within rather broad limits. Let's see how these opinions developed.

The chronology of helicopter controllability is not unlike that of fixed-wing aircraft. The writer recalls one of the Curtiss fixed-wing machines he flew in the 1930s. In the course of a normal takeoff, circuit of the field, approach, and landing, the control stick grip traveled something like 15-18 inches fore and aft! At the time, it was acceptable because I had nothing to compare. After WWII, I probably would have scared myself in that machine because I had, by then, adapted to *rapid following rates* (in this case airframe pitch or roll rates) and *high control sensitivity*. So it was with the early full-size helicopters. The two most popular small full-size machines

Fig. 5-2. Another view of the Lockheed Cheyenne showing the stub wings, pusher propeller, and tail rotor on the end of the horizontal stabilizer. The full size machine cruised using only the wings for lift. Collective pitch was full down. Thrust was provided by the propeller.

were, of course, the Bell and Hiller helicopters, each type incorporating teetering rotors with provisions for damping (the stabilizer bar on the Bell and the control rotor on the Hiller). Probably the overwhelming majority of helicopter pilots who learned to fly in the 1950s and 1960s had their early training in these machines. Both of these configurations (including the various models of each produced during that period) had relatively low control power, only moderate rotor following rates, and fairly low control sensitivity.

Let's digress a moment and I think we can get a clue to the difference in the handling characteristics between airplanes and helicopters. Although the airplane is capable of motion about all three axis, the primary motion is along only one axis with only slight components along the other two. In other words, the airplane pretty much goes the way it is pointed. The controls that accomplish motion about the three axis are essentially rate-producing controls. The moment-generating control surfaces are all far from the airplane's CG so that relatively large control moments (control power) with high damping are achieved. The helicopter, on the other hand, flies through the same three dimensions with capability of motion about and along all three axis. The possible directions and attitudes of flight, then, are infinite and motion along each axis includes both positive and negative velocities, and of course, zero. True, the controls that accomplish this are also moment generating, but pitch and roll moments are created by varying the arm offset of the relatively constant thrust or lift force in all articulated or teetering rotors. The moments generated are opposed by relatively low aerodynamic damping of the rotor blades themselves (as discussed in Chapter 4). Figure 5-3 demonstrates how a nose-up or nose-down

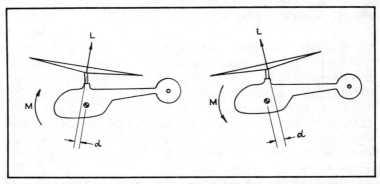

Fig. 5-3. Pitch (or roll) control power with the teetering or articulated rotor is demonstrated here. It is always L times d.

pitching moment is generated with a teetering rotor (with no flap-wise snubbing).

The moment that is available to control the helicopter is equal to the lift, or thrust, of the rotor times the offset distance—that is, $M = (L) \times (d)$. Note that if an unsnubbed teetering rotor is sitting on the ground turning at rated RPM but in flat pitch (no lift), it is not possible to generate a pitch or roll moment. This is regardless of how much cyclic input is applied because, even though the rotor is tilted, the lift is zero, and therefore, $M = (0) \times (d) = 0$!

How does this tie in with our R/C models? Well, the pioneers in R/C helicopters naturally selected the popular designs with which to experiment, namely the configurations that had evolved in the full-size machines, the two blade teetering rotor with some means of damping such as the stabilizer bar or control rotor with many variations on the theme. They are relatively simple, light-weight, and easy to rig so they quickly became the standard design (particularly the control rotor version) for almost all models, whether scratchbuilt or kitted scale type. Thus, practically all the early R/C helicopter modelers learned to fly this system, and since they had nothing with which to compare, the low control power, moderate following rate, and low sensitivity characteristic was acceptable (just as the 1930 fixed-wing machine mentioned earlier was acceptable for the same reason).

As an example of just how big a role *opinion* plays in establishing an "acceptable" following rate and control sensitivity, I might relate the following incident. I made the transition in full-size machines from teetering rotors with their moderate following rates and low control sensitivity (necessitated by poor control power with this configuration) to the Lockheed rigid rotor with high control power and sensitivity not unlike that of a WWII fighter at cruising speed. So my first R/C helicopter (a JetRanger kit) was modified to include greatly increased control power (very stiff snubber in teet-ering hinge) and also greatly increased pitch and roll sensitivity. Thus I learned to fly an R/C model with what I considered to have only marginally acceptable control power. On separate occasions, due to my lack of anything to use for comparison, I asked two well-known, highly qualified and experienced R/C helicopter fliers, with many times my experience, to fly my JetRanger and tell me what they thought. They both (without the other's knowledge) commented that the controls were all "much too sensitive!"

I do feel that, with the advent of the rigid or semi-rigid rotor and its inherent high control power, the future trend will be toward accepting higher following rates and high control sensitivity. This trend will, of course, be accompanied by a "re-educated" touch at the transmitter sticks. I think, in fact, we are already seeing this trend in the models capable of loops and rolls, and more recently, in inverted hover capability. To summarize the above: R/C helicopter models with high rotor following rates and control sensitivity are desirable from the standpoint of good maneuverability, but they will be more difficult to control (that is, to keep up with) if static and dynamic stability is poor.

CONTROLLABILITY OF A HILLER-TYPE ROTOR

As indicated earlier, the overwhelming majority of R/C helicopters presently are of the two-bladed teetering rotor type with a control rotor known as the "Hiller configuration" (Fig. 5-4). Let's follow through the controls and see how it works. Figure 5-5 shows the top and side views of the rotor in three time sequences, each 90 degrees of rotation later. We will consider a nose-down input in the example. In the upper figure, a nose-down feathering displacement has just been applied to the control rotor airfoil (a) at $\psi = 90$ degrees and a nose-up feathering displacement to (b) at $\psi = 270$ degrees. Neither the main rotor or control rotor have any flapping as yet. Because the control rotor is free to flap with essentially no restraint (see Chapter 2), the phase angle between input force and maximum flapping displacement is always 90 degrees). So 90 degrees later (II) the control surface (a), at $\psi = 180$ degrees is flapped down and surface (b), at $\psi = 0$, is flapped up. Because flapping the control rotor feathers the main rotor blades, blade (A) at $\psi = 90$ degrees, receives a nose-down feathering input and blade (B) at $\psi = 270$ degrees a nose-up input. As with the control rotor, the main rotor is also unrestrained in flapping, and therefore it too has a 90 degree phase angle between feathering input and maximum flapping. Thus when blade (A) arrives at $\psi = 180$ degrees, it is flapped down and blade (B) is flapped up at $\psi = 0$ degrees which tilts the thrust vector forward to achieve the desired nose-down response.

I think it is evident from the above that if weights are added to the control paddles (a) and (b), the control rotor takes on more authority as a stabilizing gyro to the main rotor. This will increase the period (i.e., the time) of the oscillation. Thus the helicopter is less unstable, but because the control rotor is now heavier, its following rate will be slower and therefore, the controllability will be more sluggish. What about added tip weights to the main rotor

Fig. 5-4. One of the many fine "Hiller-type" rotor heads in which the pilot "flies" the control rotor and the control rotor "flies" the main rotor.

blades? Well, the positive speed stability will be decreased somewhat, which as before increased the length of time oscillation, making the machine less dynamically unstable. The improvement in stability, however, will not be as pronounced as in the other configuration, particularly if the control rotor has 100 percent authority over the main rotor. The following rate of the gyro will be faster because it is lighter, and therefore the response will appear to be crisper with the second configuration.

PHASE ANGLE AND NUMBER OF BLADES

It would be helpful at this point to clarify a misconception one hears occasionally concerning the phase angle and the number of blades in a rotor. The phase angle is solely a function of *end fixity*, that is, the degree of flapping freedom where the blade is attached at the hub. If it is free to flap, as in a teetering rotor or a fully articulated configuration, the phase angle is *always* 90 degrees—no

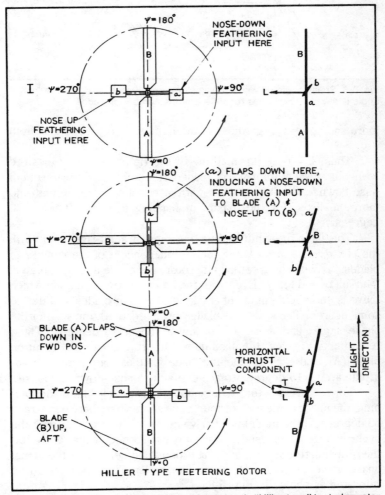

Fig. 5-5. This is a time sequence study of the classic "Hiller-type" teetering rotor after a nose-down input is applied in sequence I. Sequence II shows the resulting rotor response.

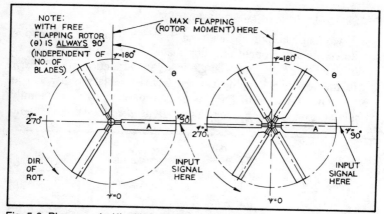

Fig. 5-6. Phase angle (θ) with flapping blades with free-flapping blades, phase angle is always 90 degrees regardless of the number of blades.

more and no less, regardless of the number of blades as shown in Fig. 5-6.

Thus, if a nose-down tilting of the tip-path-plane is desired with either the three or six bladed rotor shown, the maximum nose-down feathering input must still occur at $\psi = 90$ degrees—no more, no less, for the maximum flapping to occur at $\psi = 180$ degrees.

The same principle applies to a rigid or semi-rigid rotor with the phase angle again being totally independent of the number of blades. As with the free-flapping rotor, the phase angle is solely a function of end fixity. Even with the so-called rigid rotor, in which there is no flapping hinge of any kind, the rotor blades still flex to some degree. The stiffer the blade (low deflection), the smaller the phase angle, and it can be as low as 65 or so degrees. Thus, referring to Fig. 5-7, the maximum feathering input must occur on blade (A), and each succeeding blade for that matter, at $\psi = $ approximately 115 degrees to achieve a pure nose-down response.

For teetering rotors with snubbers that damp the blade flapping, the phase angle will, of course, be somewhere between 90 and 65 degrees. If the model is a fairly simple "bolt-together" with the cyclic linkage all exposed, it is usually a fairly simple matter to shift the swashplate non-rotating part around and determine the actual phase angle by trial and error. The bellcranks may have to be relocated as shown in Fig. 5-8.

To test, hover, the machine and give a sharp but short duration nose-up pulse. For counterclockwise turning rotors (looking down on top), if the nose-up response is accompanied by a left roll, then the swashplate must be shifted in the direction of rotor rotation. If the nose-up response is accompanied by a right roll, then of course, the non-rotating portion of the swashplate has been shifted too far in the direction of rotation and must be moved back against the direction of rotation.

FINER POINTS OF CONTROLLABILITY

Even though your new scratchbuilt helicopter may not have the best stability in the world, you, as the builder, have one final modification that is easy to make. Within reasonable limits, it can make a big difference in your ability to control the machine. This modification involves changing the control sensitivity. As stated at the beginning of this chapter, control sensitivity is, to a great extent, a matter of personal preference. When experimenting to determine what suits you, be cautious and make small changes, because they make a pussycat out of a tiger—or vice versa! Let's review how it works. Figure 5-9 is a schematic drawing of a typical cyclic control to cause a feathering input to (for example) a control rotor of a "Hiller System".

We will assume a unit length of (a) for the rotating arm of the servo which has the usual 100 degrees total travel. If we use 90 degrees or ± 45 degrees from neutral (discounting trim travel), then the linear travel from neutral, either way, will be (.707) (a).

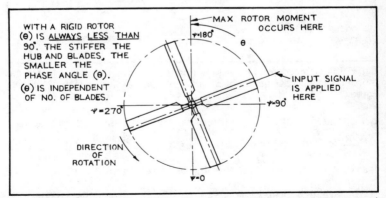

Fig. 5-7. Phase angle with rigid rotor. The rigid rotor has a much higher natural flapping frequency because it is restrained at the root (Fig. 2-7). $\frac{\Omega}{W_N}$ becomes less than one, and from Fig. 2-7 we see the phase angle between input and response is smaller. With the Lockheed Cheyenne model it was about 70 degrees in standard air (damping).

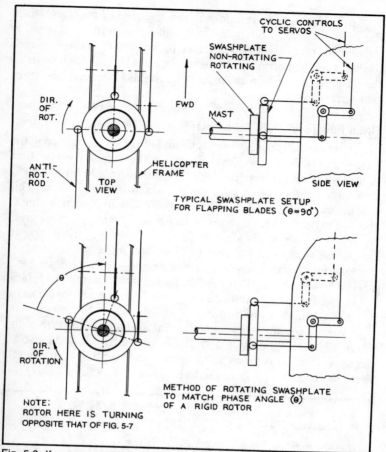

Fig. 5-8. If cross-coupling is present, (that is, with a pure nose-up input), the model responds nose-up but also with a roll. One easy cure is shown in this figure.

Now then, in Fig. 5-9, the vertical travel to the swashplate will be $\frac{2a}{a} \times (.707)$ (a) which simplifies to (1.414) (a), and the vertical travel from neutral at the blade pitch arm is (1.414) (a) $\times \frac{1.9a}{2.2a}$ which simplifies to (1.22) (a). Now then, the interesting thing here is that you can make the servo arm any convenient length. Furthermore, you know that the *vertical travel at the end of the pitch arm, in this example, will always be about 20 percent greater than the length of the pitch arm you select.*

In Fig. 5-10 *one* bellcrank has been changed to different proportions. Here, the vertical travel from neutral at the end of the blade pitch arm is $.707 (a) \times \dfrac{a}{2a} \times \dfrac{1.9a}{2.2a}$ which simplifies to .31a. The important point is that by changing the proportions of only one bellcrank we have changed the sensitivity by a factor of nearly four! If we start with Fig. 5-9 and then change to 5-10, we have decreased the sensitivity to about one fourth the original. If we had started with Fig. 5-10 and then changed to 5-9, the sensitivity would have increased by four times. The example is a rather drastic change, but was selected to demonstrate how effective it can be. Furthermore, the convenient aspect is that the modeler can make the ratio change anywhere in the system between the servo arm and the pitch arm.

One other point worth considering is the angular travel of the airfoil. Let's consider the configuration of Fig. 5-9 again in which the end of the pitch arm travels from neutral 1.22 times whatever dimension (a) is selected to be for the servo arm. Let's select (a) to be equal to .5 inch. This also fixes the length of the pitch arm as equal to $(1.90) (.5) = .95$ inches, and the actual vertical travel is $(1.22) (.5) = .61$ inch. The airfoil, pitch arm, and the vertical travel from neutral, are shown in Fig. 5-11. The angular travel is calcu-

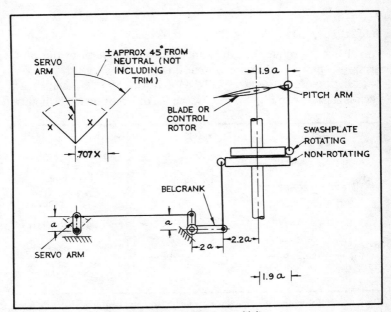

Fig. 5-9. One method of increasing control sensitivity.

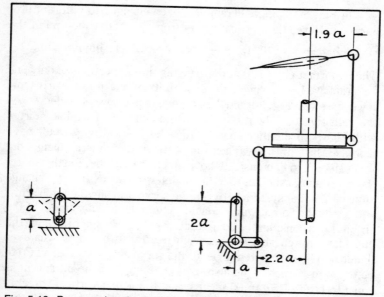

Fig. 5-10. By reversing the bellcrank going to the swashplate, the system becomes very insensitive. There are infinite combinations available to produce the control sensitivity that pleases you.

lated as ($\frac{.61}{.95}$) ×(57.3) = 36.8 degrees. This is obviously far more travel than is required. So by increasing the length of the pitch arms, we have another way to cut down on sensitivity.

Let's increase the length of the pitch arm from .95 inches to 1.5 inches as shown in Fig. 5-11. Now the maximum travel from neutral

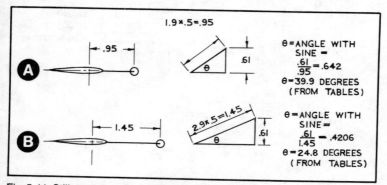

Fig. 5-11. Still one more way to vary sensitivity. Here the length of the blade pitch arm is varied.

equals $(\frac{.61}{1.50}) \times (57.3) = 23.3$ degrees. That is, by increasing the pitch arm from .95 to 1.50 inches, and with no other changes, the airfoil incidence change is reduced from 36.8 degrees to 23.3 degrees. This is a reduction in sensitivity of approximately 37 percent. The numbers are not very realistic in the example, but that matters not, as long as we can see the concept.

Chapter 6

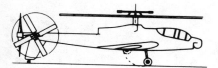

What About Stall?

This subject invariably comes up during a discussion on R/C helicopters. It is sometimes referred to as "blade-tip stall." Is it something to be concerned about? How would a model behave during a stall? How likely is an R/C model to encounter a stall? Let's begin by taking a look at what really happens in this situation. Unlike the airplane which stalls at very low speed,* the helicopter would stall in straight and level flight at high speed. Figure 6-1 is a rotating rotor that is also advancing at high speed in level flight.

Let's assume for argument that the tangential speed at the rotor tip is 300 feet per second and that the horizontal speed of the machine is 50 mph—or about 74 feet per second. Now then, the advancing blade at $\psi = 90$ degrees is actually exposed to the rotational speed plus the translational speed. The advancing tip, therefore, has a velocity of 374 feet per second, whereas the retreating blade tip at $\psi = 270$ is exposed to the rotational speed minus the translational speed, or $300 - 74 = 226$ feet per second. Thus the retreating blade tip is exposed to only about 60 percent of the advancing tip velocity. Therefore, from Chapter 2, we know that the retreating blade must have higher angles of attack than the advancing blade, to make up for the reduction in speed. This, of course, is achieved by the application of cyclic pitch control.

As the forward speed continues to increase due to more forward cyclic pitch, the retreating blade has lower and lower net

---

*Excepting "secondary" or high speed stalls during G turns or pullups.

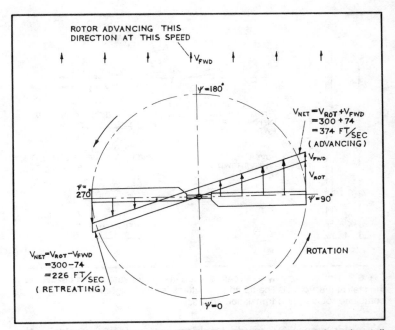

Fig. 6-1. This is similar to Fig. 2-2, but is repeated here to study it from the stall viewpoint. Again, notice the advancing blade has a much higher velocity than the retreating blade.

velocity and higher and higher angles of attack. If the engine is powerful enough and the parasite drag is low enough, eventually the forward speed increases to the point where the angles of attack is so high that the retreating blade stalls. But what part of the blade stalls first? To answer this, we must realize that as inflow down through the rotor increases (due to forward flight increase), the point at which the blade airfoil has the maximum angle of attack shifts outboard towards the *tip* of the blade. Figure 6-2 shows a rotor blade and the airfoil at two blade stations. The blade has zero twist, so that with zero inflow, the angle of attack is the same as the pitch angle (θ) for both blade stations.

Now at the right side of the figure, an inflow velocity (ν) has been added to both section stations r_1 and r_2. Because of the higher tangential speed at r_2, the *angle of attack* ($\propto$) is greater at the tip than inboard. The stall, therefore, first begins at the tip, hence the term *tip stall*.

Referring back to Fig. 6-1, our initial impression is that the stall would first appear at the azimuth position of 270 degrees, ie.,

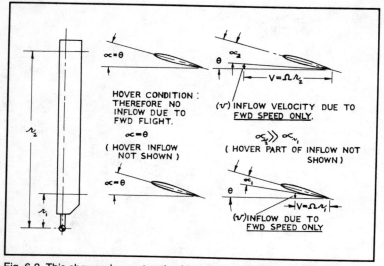

Fig. 6-2. This shows why a retreating blade in high forward speed always feels the stall at the *tip* first. The tip angle of attack is much higher due to the slower combined rotation and translation speed.

the point where we would think the net velocity would be the lowest. Because the inflow is approaching and being drawn down through the rotor at a very shallow slant, however, experience with full-size machines on which this entire discussion is based indicates that the highest angles of attack consequently occur at ψ equal to approximately 300 degrees.

Figure 6-3 is a typical angle of attack contour plot. The shaded area near the tip around the azimuth of 300 degrees, i.e., from about 270 to about 315 degrees, represents the onset of the blade tip stall. This contour is based on a constant chord, untwisted blade using an airfoil that would stall above about 13 or 14 degrees, which represent the vast majority of our models. The stall would begin with very little warning. Rotor vibration (which the modeler would not see, of course) would increase quite rapidly as the airflow would separate from the blade and then reattach itself to the blade once each revolution. The vibration is caused by the very high drag during the stalled part of the revolution. This drag tends to reduce the RPM, which propagates the condition. From level straight flight, the result would be a rather sudden nose-up-pitch accompanied by roll toward the advancing blade! Why the roll? If we recall, the blade would have a sudden loss of lift at ψ = about 300 degrees. Now then, remember that the maximum flapping, in this case *down*, would occur at ψ = about 30 degrees which would cause nose-up and roll.

HOW LIKELY IS AN R/C MODEL TO ENCOUNTER STALL?

Answering the topic question properly requires some very sophisticated mathematics which are beyond this discussion. We can, however, get a surprisingly accurate picture of just how close

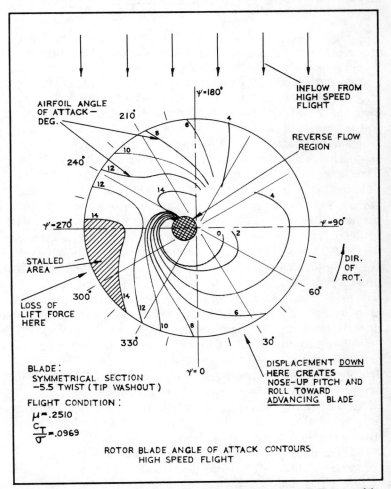

Fig. 6-3. A typical polar contour of a rotor well into the blade stall. The top of the circle is the forward point of the helicopter. The contour lines connect areas which have the same angle of attack. Notice that the shaded area is the stalled portion of the blade.

an R/C model would be to the threshold of stall for any given set of flight parameters. There are trends of two basic aerodynamic dimensionless relationships that would be always present at the onset to a stall. Namely:

$$\text{High advance ratio } \mu = \frac{V \cos \alpha}{\Omega R}$$

$$\text{High ratio of } \frac{\text{Thrust Coefficient}}{\text{Rotor Solidity}} = \frac{C_T}{\sigma}$$

Figure 6-4 is a plot of (μ) versus (C_T/σ), in which the slanted line represents the combination of values of these quantities that would be present at the threshold of the stall. All points below the shaded areas represent essentially zero probability of stall occurring for all but the very worst models. The lightly shaded band represents the threshold of stall for models having twisted blades (5-8 degrees) and a superior blade airfoil for which the stall occurs at a high angle of attack (16-18 degrees). The heavy shaded portion represents probability of severe stall for even the optimum design. The curves of Fig. 6-4 were derived from actual flight test data of full-size machines. These data, then, (RPM, speed, rotor size, weight, etc.) were reduced to R/C model size parameters by a mathematical procedure known as *dynamic similarity*. From this mathematical procedure, scale performance could be determined for the R/C model. From the scale performance, values of (μ) and (C_T/σ) were calculated which represented the stall thresholds. The procedure is valid, incidentally, because both (μ) and (C_T/σ) are dimensionless, as earlier stated, and dynamic similarity reduces to unity for both (μ) and (C_T/σ) and therefore, they could be plotted directly from the full size machine flight test data. Our R/C helicopters fly in "actual" air which has slightly higher *relative viscosity* than "scale" air, which makes the actual Reynolds Number, N_R, slightly lower than scale N_R (from dynamic similarity). The error, however, is reasonably small, and because the actual N_R at which our R/C blades operate, has a little lower stall angle (by about one degree) than for the "scale" N_R (for most airfoils), feel that the data of Fig. 6-4 is slightly conservative.

In our quest to answer the topic question, let's first examine the two relationships to determine what they contain:

advance ratio $\boxed{\mu = \frac{V \cos \alpha}{\Omega R}}$ where:

V = helicopter speed-feet/sec
Ω = rotor rotation speed

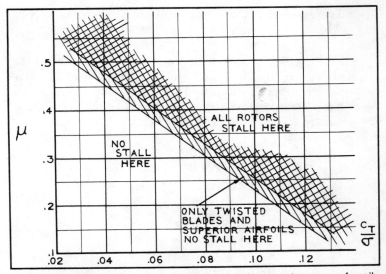

Fig. 6-4. This graph is an emperical but surprisingly accurate means of easily estimating the onset of the stall. See the text for the method.

thrust coefficient = C_T

$$C_T = \frac{T}{\pi R^2 \rho (\Omega R)^2}$$

$= \frac{\text{RPM} \times 2\pi}{60} - \text{radians/sec}$

$\propto$ = rotor angle of attack

T = rotor thrust = helicopter weight-lbs

π = constant = 3.14

R = rotor radius-ft

ρ = air density .0024

b = number of blades

c = blade chord-ft

solidity = $\sigma = \dfrac{bc}{\pi R}$

therefore $\dfrac{C_T}{\sigma} = \dfrac{T \pi R}{\pi R^2 \rho (\Omega R)^2 bc}$ note: the term (ΩR) is the tangential speed of the rotor tip

simplified, $\boxed{\dfrac{C_T}{\sigma} = \dfrac{T}{R \rho (\Omega R)^2 bc}}$

Advance Ratio: Note here that either a high forward speed (v) or a low rotor speed (Ω) will contribute to the stall condition. $\dfrac{\text{(THRUST COEFFICIENT)}}{\text{ROTOR SOLIDITY}}$: In the expression for C_T/σ there appears the term T/Rcb which is the blade loading. Therefore, a high

77

blade loading—and again in this expression a low rotor speed, indeed here it is the square of the rotor speed (Ω^2) that aggravate the stall!

Using Fig. 6-4, let's calculate the airspeed for the threshold to the stall for, say, a .61 size JetRanger. The approach to the problem will be to calculate (C_T/σ), then go to the lower line of Fig. 6-4 and read off the corresponding value of (μ). From (μ) then, we calculate the predicted speed of the threshold of the stall. Assume:

$$
\begin{aligned}
W &= T = 11.5 \text{ lbs} \\
\Omega &= 950 \text{ RPM of rotor} \\
&= \frac{950 \times 2\pi}{60} = 99.5 \text{ radians/sec} \\
R &= 31 \text{ inches} = 2.58 \text{ ft} \\
\rho &= .0024 \text{ slugs/ft} \\
b &= 2 \text{ blades} \\
c &= 2\tfrac{1}{4} \text{ inches} = .187 \text{ ft} \\
\Omega R &= (99.5)(2.58) = 256.7 \\
(\Omega R)^2 &= 65900 \\
\propto &= \text{rotor angle of attack} \\
&= \text{about 15 degrees nose-down} \\
&\quad \cos 15 \text{ degrees} = .965
\end{aligned}
$$

Then $\dfrac{C_T}{\sigma} = \dfrac{T}{R\,\rho\,(\Omega R)^2\,bc} = \dfrac{11.5}{(2.58)(.0024)(65900)(2)(.187)} = .075$

From Fig. 6-4, $\mu = .325$ for $\dfrac{C_T}{\sigma} = .075$

Now then $\qquad \mu = \dfrac{V \cos \propto}{\Omega R}$ or $V = \dfrac{(\mu)(\Omega R)}{\cos \propto}$

$V = \dfrac{(.325)(256.7)}{.965} = 86.5$ feet per second (59 mph).

CONCLUSION

From the above calculations, then, it is concluded that only models with exceptionally powerful engines, and with very large rotors (six feet diameter and up) turning at low RPM (for high hover efficiency) would ever operate near the stall threshold. I have seen a number of "whing-dings" that were attributed to blade tip stall, which were, in fact, due to other causes. The most common is nose-up pitch due to negative angle of attack stability during a power reduction. The thought may occur to you that a pullup from a high speed dive in which a high load is developed would trigger a retreating blade tip stall. This is not the case, because although it is true the effective weight, and therefore (C_T/σ), will increase, the pullout which induces the G load is accomplished by aft cyclic control. This *reduces* the angle of attack on the retreating blade before the G load develops, thereby reducing the chance for stall to begin. The same thinking, incidentally, applies to a steep high G turn. Again the retreating blade is taken out of the high angle of attack condition by the constant aft cyclic. Besides, it would be very difficult, if not impossible, to maintain very high speed in, say, 2G (60 degrees) bank turn! If retreating blade stall *is* ever encountered during a high speed dash, *do not* apply forward cyclic control to combat the pitch-up. This would merely aggravate the stall with a still higher angle of attack on the retreating blade. The correct recovery is to roll toward the retreating blade and reduce collective control, if so equipped.

There is one other flight regime where I think it may be possible to actually experience blade stall, even with the smaller .40 size helicopters. There have been cases in the recovery from a loop that the machine sometimes tends to roll during the recovery dive. Let's see how this might happen. Unlike the fixed-wing machine which maintains full thrust capability completely around the loop, thus making the loop a fairly respectable circle, the helicopter rotor applies a decelerating thrust vector with nose-up moment. Consider the model in Fig. 6-5. At the left of the figure, the

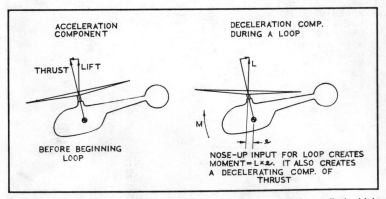

Fig. 6-5. When a model starts into a loop, nose-down pitch is applied which carries with it an accelerating component of speed. As the loop begins, aft cyclic is applied which brings the nose up but also decelerates the forward speed, making round loops difficult in a helicopter.

model is accelerating in a nose-down attitude because the horizontal component of thrust is forward. At the right side of Fig. 6-5 aft cyclic has been applied to tilt the rotor aft, to bring the nose-up to execute the loop. In so doing, however, a decelerating thrust component causes a rapid loss of speed, particularily with the smaller light-weight machines. Because of the relatively low momentum and the aft pointing vector during the loop, many of the loops are similar in shape to that of Fig. 6-6. Because of the rapid deceleration, the helicopter speed is very low as the machine rotates at the top and begins its downward plunge. If the loop is started at only a moderate altitude, the tendency will be to rotate the machine nose-up while yet in a very high sink rate, and if the model is getting close to the ground, add power here and the stage is all set! With this combination of high sink rate, low forward speed, and added power, the model is very near the "vortex ring" state of recirculation discussed in Chapter 3 except here there is some forward speed but a much higher sink rate. Thus the rotor blades are operating at very high angles of attack around the azimuth.

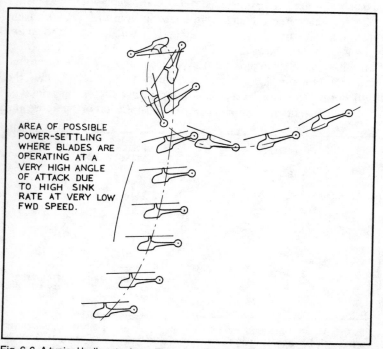

AREA OF POSSIBLE POWER-SETTLING WHERE BLADES ARE OPERATING AT A VERY HIGH ANGLE OF ATTACK DUE TO HIGH SINK RATE AT VERY LOW FWD SPEED.

Fig. 6-6. A typical helicopter loop. The descent can give rise to a stall when the air is disturbed as it flows up past the canopy.

It is my opinion (nothing more) that as the blade is passing over the canopy, the inflow is momentarily disturbed due to turbulence, and the blade stalls at the forward azimuth position. This loss of lift is felt as a downward force at $\psi = 180$ degrees. The flow re-attaches after it passes the canopy. The displacement on these teetering rotors, of course, occurs 90 degrees later. With a clockwise turning rotor, therefore, the rotor tip-path-plane displaces down at about $\psi = 270$ degrees which would produce a right roll (toward the retreating blade). I understand that, in the recovery from a loop if the model does roll, it rolls toward the retreating blade.

Chapter 7

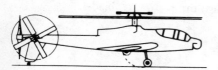

Autorotation

How can I be reasonably sure my R/C helicopter will autorotate without finding out the hard way? What about blade angles, clutches, and so forth?

The very first thing to do is to be sure we know what we mean when we use the term *autorotation*. In general, we know that when power is expended to turn the rotor shaft rapidly, lift will result if the blades are set at a positive angle of attack. Therefore, it seems reasonable that if power to the shaft is removed (engine stops) and the blades are shifted to a negative blade angle, the upflow of air through the rotor as the machine descends will continue to turn the rotor to produce lift. Hence we have autorotation. The above is a true statement but it doesn't tell the whole story. All rotors will autorotate to one degree or another. At one end of the spectrum we have a rotor with high negative pitch angles operating at a relatively low speed, high torque condition but offering relatively low resistance to the inflowing air. This end of the spectrum is referred to as the *windmilling state*. Until fairly recently, most R/C helicopter rotors were in the windmill state, power off. I recall my "initiation." The beast was flying toward me at about 30 feet altitude and about 20 mph when, without warning, the engine came unglued (wrist pin failure)—full down collective and then a whole bunch of inputs, none of which made any sense because it had already fallen onto the ground, bouncing once or twice. I don't think a brick could have made it much faster! It wasn't true autorotation but was actually a classic case of rotor windmilling.

Now let's back up and conduct a little experiment and I think we will uncover the basic requirements that *must* be present to experience true autorotation. All that is needed for this experiment is an R/C tail rotor assembly mounted on a shaft with two ball bearings and a means whereby the pitch can be adjusted by hand with a pushrod or whatever, and an electric fan. Start the fan and hold the tail rotor in front with the blades at a steep pitch angle as shown in Fig. 7-1. The rotor will begin to turn due to the air inflow and the direction of rotation will be clockwise looking into the end of the rotor (nearest blade traveling up). Now while in this condition, notice that the rotor assembly seems to offer little resistance to the blowing air but that if you touch the shaft the rotor *is* developing a strong torque. This is the windmill state.

Now, without any other change, slowly *reduce* or flatten the pitch angle of the tail rotor blades as shown in Fig. 7-2 and notice the response. Your tail rotor will take off to a much higher RPM with tremendous acceleration. Furthermore, you will now notice a definite resistance tending to push the high speed rotating rotor away from the fan (here is the lift we so desperately need to slow the descent). This is the autorotation state. You do not, however, get off scot-free—rest your finger against the high speed shaft and I think

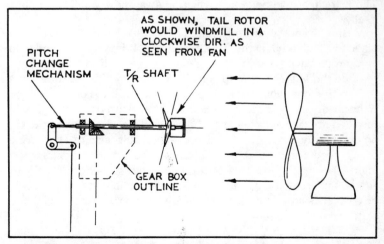

Fig. 7-1. This is an experiment you can try with a tail rotor and gearbox. Here the blades are set to accelerate into rotation from the fan air.

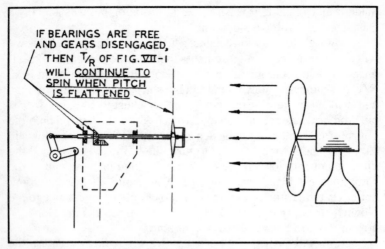

Fig. 7-2. When the tail rotor in Fig. 7-1 stabilizes, adjust the pitch to a flat position as shown. It will rotate much faster and you will feel resistance from the air. This is true autorotation. The condition of Fig. 7-1 is called "windmilling."

you will find it takes very little drag to slow the rotation down because it is developing very little torque. Now, go one step further. Without changing the blade pitch, apply enough friction to the shaft to stop the rotor and then release the friction. Notice anything strange? The rotor that had been just whizzing away now won't even start itself will it?

Here is another little goodie. Go back to the first step, set the blade to a high pitch in the fan stream to get it into motion, and then play around with the pitch angle until it sounds like you have reached the highest RPM. Then slowly remove the tail rotor from the airstream without changing pitch and allow it to come to a stop. If the airfoil is low drag, has a clean surface, sharp trailing edge, and the shaft drag is not excessive, you will find that the blade angle will be essentially *flat*, i.e., zero degrees. Furthermore, if you have a really good rotor—that is, a blade whose lift-over-drag is *very* high—the angle will be back the other way by as much as a degree or so! To understand how this seemingly incredible statement could be true, let's now go back and compare a main rotor in the windmill state versus the autorotative state.

Notice that in the windmill state of Fig. 7-3, the blade incidence is required to be set to a steep negative angle so that the resultant (R) of the lift and drag forces tilt forward. This produces a component of thrust (T) in the direction of rotation. This must be true when the rotor is required to overcome an appreciable internal torque load in the form of gears, belts, bearing friction, etc. The horizontal component will accelerate the rotor rotation only until the T force exactly equals the blades' skin friction plus the internal torque load. At this point, equilibrium will be established because the net force is zero, and the RPM will remain constant. Notice particularly in Fig. 7-3 the relatively small angle of attack ($\propto$) that is available to produce lift.

Now shift your glassy gaze to Fig. 7-4 which is a similar rotor except that this one is not carrying an internal load. It has been disconnected from the power train, insofar as is possible, by a "one-way" cam-roller clutch. Figure 7-4 is a blade in the true autoritative state. Notice that the resultant lies on the axis of rotation which means that, as in the other figure, the rotor speed is stabilized but here at a much higher RPM. Furthermore, notice that the section chordline is actually at a positive incidence (θ) and even more importantly, the blade angle of attack ($\propto$) is much greater than it is in the windmill state. Thus, with this rotor a nice slow "glide-like" rate of descent is possible. Yes, it *can* happen to a R/C helicopter. I have seen one that did glide reasonably slowly.

WHAT MODIFICATIONS ARE NEEDED?

There are several things we can consider which will help the rotor to achieve the autorotative state rather than the windmill condition.

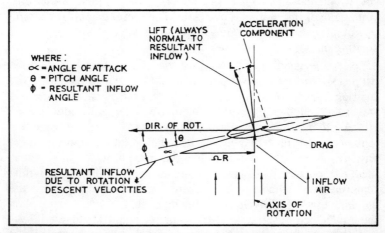

Fig. 7-3. This is a diagram of a blade in the windmill state. The angle of attack to product lift ($\propto$) is very small.

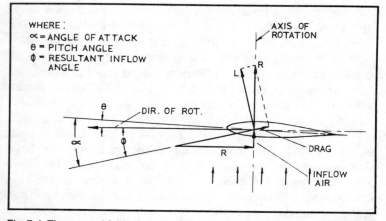

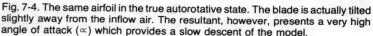

Fig. 7-4. The same airfoil in the true autorotative state. The blade is actually tilted slightly away from the inflow air. The resultant, however, presents a very high angle of attack (∝) which provides a slow descent of the model.

Reduce resistance to free turning. Install a one-way cam-roller clutch on the main rotor shaft. If the clutch is above the T/R takeoff point, this will provide the absolute minimum resistance but at a sacrifice of loss of directional control. If the clutch is below the tail rotor takeoff point then the model will still be directionally controllable but the model will have a higher sink rate because of lower RPM. In either case, be sure that all bearing alignment is good and all shafts turn freely with oil. A note of caution here: There are a couple of compact and lightweight over-running clutches which are, I understand, commercially available. The secret to their successful operation lies in maintaining accurately aligned and supported shafting on both sides of the clutch.

Another good way to overcome the friction torque of the drive train is to go to a three or four bladed rotor which increases the rotational driving force (Fig. 7-5). Whether the advantage gained is worth the added complexity is for the modeler to decide.

Another helpful modification is to add weight to the blade tips to improve the rotor momentum. If the autorotation begins at a high altitude, the weights will not alter the RPM at which the rotor is finally stabilized. The weights, however, will increase the time required to stabilize the RPM, and if a model tends toward the windmill state, the added time may be enough to get the model on the ground before the sink rate becomes too high due to low RPM.

Other than very low shaft friction torque, the other real secret to true autorotation is an accurate blade contour of a very high lift-to-drag ratio airfoil, sharp trailing edges, and smooth waxed surfaces.

AUTOROTATION ENTRY AND LANDING: BASIC PROCEDURE

First of all, forget any attempts at autorotation entry from *all* altitudes between about three feet and about 25 feet (or more) unless the model has a pretty fair forward speed—say above about 15 mph. At low speed within the above altitude limits, the model is too high to get into the ground before the rotor RPM decays to the windmill state, but it is too low to have time to lower the collective, build rotor RPM back up to normal, and establish a steady, slow rate of autorotation descent for a safe landing.

At first sign of an engine failure (or for an intentional entry) with adequate altitude and airspeed, immediately lower collective full down to zero degrees incidence (rig to this when building the model). At the same time the collective control is smartly lowered to full down, forward cyclic should be applied to point the nose-down. The purpose of both of these control inputs is to restore the lost rotor RPM, which occurs incredibly fast at engine failure. The degree of nose-down input and the length of time this attitude is maintained will, of course, depend on the entry conditions. If the model is in high speed level flight at failure, the nose-down attitude will be minimal in degree and time. As the RPM builds up, the machine is established in a glide altitude with a forward speed

Fig. 7-5. This model is capable of real autorotation because of the four main rotor blades.

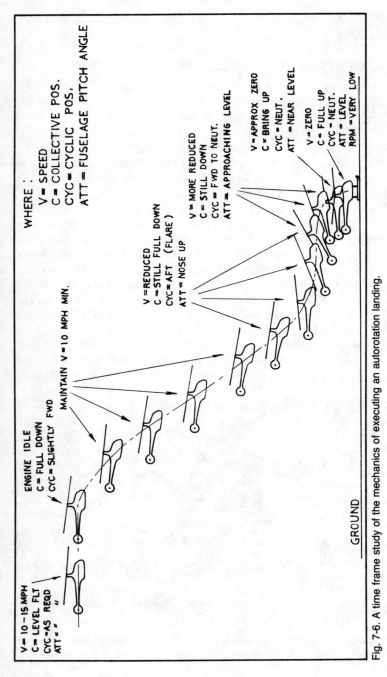

V = 10-15 MPH
C = LEVEL FLT
CYC = AS REQD
ATT = "   "

ENGINE IDLE
C = FULL DOWN
CYC = SLIGHTLY FWD

MAINTAIN V = 10 MPH MIN.

V = REDUCED
C = STILL FULL DOWN
CYC = AFT (FLARE)
ATT = NOSE UP

V = MORE REDUCED
C = STILL DOWN
CYC = FWD TO NEUT.
ATT = APPROACHING LEVEL

V = APPROX ZERO
C = BRING UP
CYC = NEUT.
ATT = NEAR LEVEL

V = ZERO
C = FULL UP
CYC = NEUT.
ATT = LEVEL
RPM = VERY LOW

WHERE :
V = SPEED
C = COLLECTIVE POS.
CYC = CYCLIC POS.
ATT = FUSELAGE PITCH ANGLE

GROUND

Fig. 7-6. A time frame study of the mechanics of executing an autorotation landing.

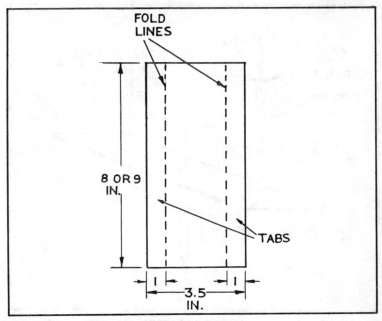

Fig. 7-7. Paper airfoil pattern for autorotation toy.

somewhere near 10 mph. See point x in Fig. 3-7, which will be near the speed for least power required, and consequently, the slowest rate of descent. As the model nears the ground (three feet), apply aft cyclic control to flare. This cyclic flare slows the forward speed and also (due to rotor angle of attack) somewhat slows the rate of descent. As the model approaches zero ground speed (nose high attitude), push the nose over to a level attitude with forward cyclic and simultaneously come up with collective control as needed, and the machine settles to the ground. If the rotor is truly in the autorotative state, the RPM will be high, and the rate of descent will be slow enough that a very gentle touchdown can be consistently accomplished. Sound easy? Well, it's like everything else—it takes a little practice. I assure you it's nowhere near as difficult as hovering inverted! Figure 7-6 is a time-frame study of the above described steps.

I'd like to complete this section with a little fun project. Obtain a piece of stiff writing paper about 3.5 inches by 8 or 9 inches. Crease as shown in Fig. 7-7. Now bend the sheet into a smooth curved surface with the two one-inch flaps overlapping, and glue them in this overlapped position as shown in Fig. 7-8.

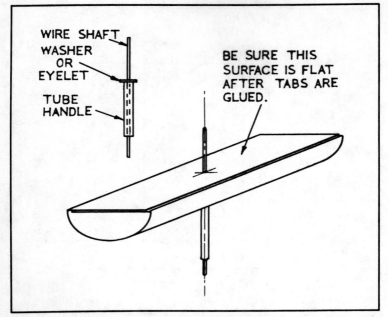

Fig. 7-8. Autorotation toy is assembled as shown.

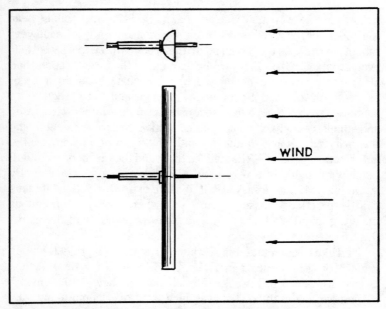

Fig. 7-9. Deployment of autorotation toy. See text for details.

You should now have a half of a cylinder (more or less). Obtain a piece of wire about 2-3 inches long; any diameter (even a coat hanger is fine), and a washer for a thrust bearing. Measure, mark, and puncture holes in the center of the flat surface and then on through the curved portion. Be sure the wire enters the flat surfaces at right angles on both axes. When complete it should look like Fig. 7-9.

Now comes the fun. Don't try this by yourself; you may become fascinated and drive up a tree. Have someone drive the car about 5-8 mph and you hold it out the window with the *flat* surface toward the oncoming wind. "Big deal," you say, "nothing happens." Oh? Give it a good flip (like starting a gas model engine) and watch it accelerate to a high RPM! Now stop the rotation and flip it the opposite direction and watch it accelerate again to a high RPM, only this time in the opposite direction from the first time. How about that, sports fans! We have here exactly the same concept as in Fig. 7-4 in which the lift vector leans forward just enough to overcome the "blade" drag to permit high speed rotation.

Although this is an amusing toy, the airfoil (curved surface) has a poor lift-to-drag ratio; yet the device rather dramatically demonstrates the concept of pure autorotation.

Chapter 8

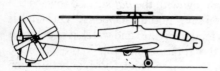

Rotor Configurations

Two blades, four blades, teetering, fully articulated, rigid rotor. What is the best configuration? Well, there probably is no *one* best configuration for all purposes—or at least it hasn't yet been found. It is assumed you are considering the various rotor configurations with the question, "What kind of rotor system should I use in my new scratchbuilt R/C model?" The objective of this section, therefore, is to list all the probable configurations you might consider, and to discuss the advantages and disadvantages of each (Fig. 8-1 through 8-3).

THE FULLY ARTICULATED ROTOR

The term *articulated*, as used here, means jointed such that each blade is free to rotate about all three axes—feathering, flapping, and lead-lag. The flapping axis may pass through the axis of rotation as in Fig. 8-4, or it may be displaced away from the axis of rotation as in Fig. 8-5. In this case the rotor is said to have an offset flapping axis, and it is, by far the most commonly used with articulated heads.

Advantages of Fig. 8-5. (for an R/C model)
   ☐ None that are apparent

Disadvantages of Fig. 8-5.
   ☐ This configuration has inherently poor control power and also low rotor damping which makes this configuration very difficult to control.

Fig. 8-1. How about this for a model rotor? It is a very large Russian helicopter.

☐ It is also limited to only two blades.

Advantages of the offset hinge articulated rotor.

    ☐ It has better control power and also better following rate than a teetering rotor, but not as good as a rigid rotor.

    ☐ It can be used with any number of blades from two up.

Figure 8-6 is an offset hinge flapping rotor. The angles are somewhat exaggerated to demonstrate how the offset hinge creates a moment to improve control power and following rate. In the

Fig. 8-2. A JetRanger control system modified to include a scissors to permit collective input without affecting cyclic control.

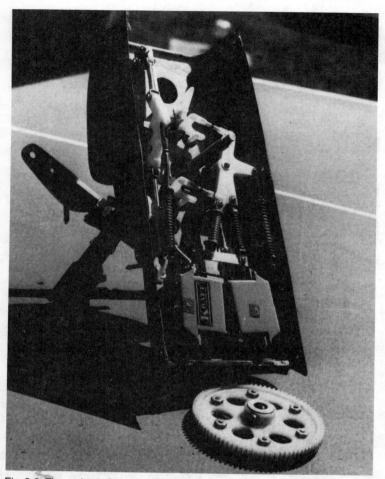

Fig. 8-3. The author's Cheyenne cyclic control system. This is the same concept (positive/negative spring force system) used on the full-size machines.

illustration the CG has been place aft, which would produce a very tail-heavy model. If the flapping hinge had been located on the rotational axis, the only control power available to overcome the effect of the aft CG would be the thrust (T) times the distance (d). With the offset hinge, however, the centrifugal force has a component along the blades which will tend to bring the hub into alignment with the blades. The moment (M) created by the CF on the offset hinge hub adds appreciable control power so that in Fig. 8-6 the total control power is $(T) \times (d) + M$.

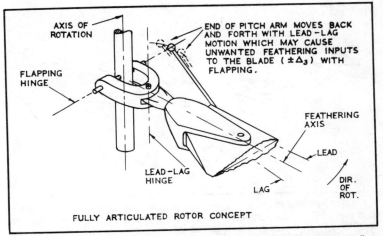

FULLY ARTICULATED ROTOR CONCEPT

Fig. 8-4. The classic fully articulated rotor blade; it has complete freedom to flap, move in-plane (lead-lag), and feather about the quarter chord axis.

Disadvantages of the offset hinge articulated rotor.

☐ The added complexity and weight of the lead-lag hinge can hardly be justified in an R/C model. In-plane (lead-lag) hinges, however, are very necessary on large full-size machines to alleviate the heavy in-plane forces which would otherwise propagate down into the airframe.

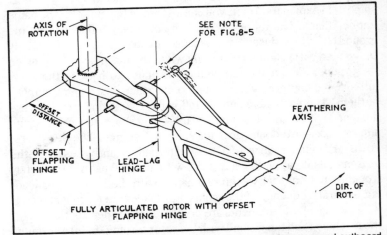

FULLY ARTICULATED ROTOR WITH OFFSET FLAPPING HINGE

Fig. 8-5. Same as Fig. 8-4 except that the flap hinge has been moved outboard from the rotor shaft, or offset. This configuration with lead-lag dampers is used on all large multibladed rotors. It is a poor choice for models.

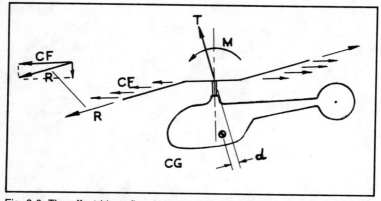

Fig. 8-6. The offset hinge flapping rotor has considerably more control power than that of Fig. 8-4. Control power to pitch is the usual T times d *plus* the centrifugal force which tries to align the rotor.

☐ Under certain conditions this configuration might be subject to ground resonance.

It is necessary to digress momentarily to clarify the subject of ground resonance, about which there are popular misconceptions.

GROUND RESONANCE

Sound familiar? Many people can explain all about it, but few understand it. Let's look into it and then the next time you hear some wild explanation of it, you can just smile to yourself. The name implies that it has its origin or is in some way influenced by the ground. It is introduced here because it can *only* occur with a fully articulated rotor, and further, *only* when the machine is running on the ground. To get the full picture we must go back to the early full-size helicopters, when ground reasonance destroyed a number of them. The early helicopters, following fixed-wing trends, were designed with nice soft landing gears—long shock absorbing struts and low pressure donut tires for smooth landings. The designers, however, didn't realize that they had inadvertantly designed the airframe, as it sat on the soft gear, with a lateral natural frequency (rocking motion) that was in resonance with the in-plane, or lead-lag, natural frequency of the main rotor blades. Let's consider Fig. 8-7 in which all the elements are present for total destruction. In (a) the machine is on the ground with the rotor turning. In (b) a stimulus is introduced. The disturbance can originate from a number of sources such as a pilot shifting in his seat or, as in the figure, a passenger steps on the tire, reaches up, and pulls himself in. If the lead-lag frequency is twice the natural roll frequency of the airframe and landing gear on the ground, the slightest disturbance will trigger the resonate condition. Once excited, these two motions—the in-plane and the airframe lateral rocking on the ground—will rapidly reinforce one another with very great amplification. Notice that going from time frame (b) to (d) represents one cycle of airframe rocking and one revolution of the rotor, but two cycles of lead-lag in-plane motion. It should also be pointed out that the fore and aft motion of the mast due to this "two per rev" in-plane is just as intense as it is laterally. The nose-up and down-pitch natural frequency of the airfarme is much lower though, and so there is little or no resonant reinforcement, and therefore no amplification on this axis.

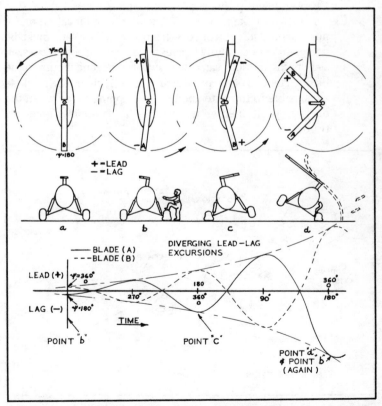

Fig. 8-7. The little-understood "ground resonance" phenomenon. The lower curves are time sequences of the blade tips divergence to destruction.

To get away from the problem, landing gears were redesigned to be very stiff and highly damped so that the roll, or lateral, rocking natural frequency was raised to a value far above the rotational or the in-plane frequencies so as to avoid resonance. Furthermore, in-plane dampers were installed on each blade to snub the lead-lag motion. This modification was intended not only for ground resonance correction, but also to alleviate excessive in-plane excursions which can be encountered with undamped articulated rotors in high speed flight.

Other disadvantages of the articulate rotor.

☐ There is the need for individual droop-stops at each flapping hinge to prevent the rotor blade from striking the tail boom during low RPM operation (start-up and shut-down). No up-stops, however, are needed because CF as we saw in Chapter 1 will prevent over-coning.

☐ The control linkage including geometry and location of the pitch arm, and control rods from the swashplate must be designed very carefully because the lead-lag action, as well as flapping motion, can cause unwanted cyclic inputs to the blade. The end of the pitch arm, Fig. 8-4, should be as close as possible to the extension of the flapping hinge when the blade is positioned as it would be for a steady hover attitude.

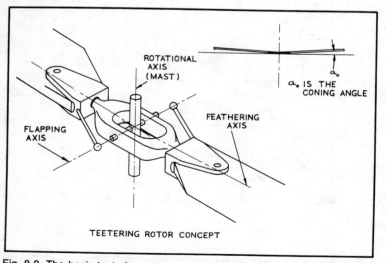

Fig. 8-8. The basic teetering rotor concept. The blades feather on a straight-through hinge that permits teeter but no in-plane action.

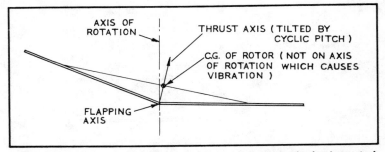

Fig. 8-9. Teetering rotor is very simple, but has the drawback of going out-of-balance when it flaps.

THE TEETERING ROTOR

The teetering or "seesaw" rotor is by far the most popular basic configuration used on R/C models. It is relatively simple, lightweight, and inexpensive to fabricate. Figure 8-8 is a sketch of the basic concept. A one-piece hub extends from one blade across to the other, and the hub is pinned to the shaft so as to transmit torque from the shaft to the hub and at the same time permit freedom of flapping movement. The blades are attached to the hub by spindles and bearings which permit the blades to be feathered for cyclic and collective pitch if so equipped. Thus, unlike the articulated designs, the assembly is very stiff in the lead-lag mode.

The teetering rotor as shown in Fig. 8-8, however, would have serious vibration problems. The vibration is caused by an imbalance created whenever the rotor flaps as shown in Fig. 8-9. The coning is exaggerated for clarity. The midpoint of a line connecting the effective CG of the two blades is the CG of the entire rotor assembly; when it flaps, the rotor CG shifts away from the axis of rotation causing an in-plane vibration that could be intense enough to bend the main rotor shaft.

The vibration problem can be greatly alleviated by introducing the "underslung hub" as shown in Fig. 8-10. In effect, it raises the teetering axis* so that dynamically, the rotor is balanced as much as possible regardless of flapping. I said *greatly alleviated* because the blades deflect with varying spanwise airloads and therefore the coning changes and the CG of the rotor assembly moves around somewhat. Thus the amount of "underslung" used is a best estimate of where the average location of the rotor CG will be in flight. Figure 8-11 is the "underslung" modification of the teetering hub.

---

*See Chapter 9 on how much to raise the teeter axis.

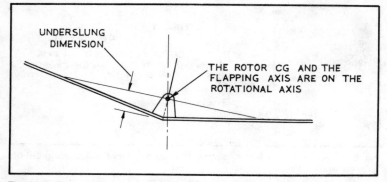

UNDERSLUNG
DIMENSION

THE ROTOR CG AND THE
FLAPPING AXIS ARE ON THE
ROTATIONAL AXIS

Fig. 8-10. The "unbalance when flapped" is corrected by using what is called an "underslung" hub such the rotor teeters about the CG of the entire rotor (or near it). The CG is constantly moving slightly due to blade deflection as the forces vary.

Advantages of the teetering rotor.

☐ Lightweight, simple construction.
☐ No possibility of ground resonance.

Disadvantages of the teetering rotor.

☐ This configuration is very difficult to fly. The rotor has poor damping in pitch and roll which aggravates both the short period and the pheugoid oscillations. The "people-pod," which dangles freely beneath the rotor, adds inputs to the rotor which further accentuates the instability.
☐ This rotor has inherently poor control power.
☐ The cyclic servos must be powerful enough to hold on input against high blade dynamic and aerodynamic feathering loads.

THE TEETERING ROTOR MODIFIED

The disadvantages with the basic teetering rotor listed above, have some straightforward solutions. These can be rather easily incorporated into the system and the teetering rotor becomes quite docile. The fixes include adding a *control rotor* which acts as a servo by which feathering inputs are applied to the main rotor. This increases pitch and roll damping because the control rotor acts somewhat like a rate gyro. Furthermore, feathering the control rotor requires far less servo power than direct control of the blade pitch. The poor control power, and to some extent the instability due to the fuselage dangling, can be alleviated by installing some kind of mechanical resistance to main rotor flapping such as a rubber snubber or springs, or both.

Figure 8-12 is a sketch of a Hiller rotor head. Notice the universal joint to which the "underslung" main rotor is attached to the shaft. Because of the universal joint, the rotational axis always tilts with the rotor. Consequently there is no cyclic feathering between the blades and the hub. Some of the smaller (.40 size) R/C models without collective control use this arrangement very successfully. The particular attraction is that the blades can be rigidly attached without even any feather bearings.

Notice also that the actual Hiller rotor head includes a control rotor that maintains 100 percent authority over the main rotor. That is, the control rotor flapping is directly connected to the main rotor feathering with no mixing link. Now we come to an important point that is sometimes overlooked. It is difficult to build an R/C model "Hiller type" rotor head that has both collective pitch and a control rotor that maintains 100 percent authority (i.e., 5 degrees control rotor flapping equal 5 degrees main rotor feathering) over the main rotor. The full-size machine has a collective push rod that runs up through the hollow main rotor shaft and then connects to the fork pitch arms. This arrangement would be too complex for our models.

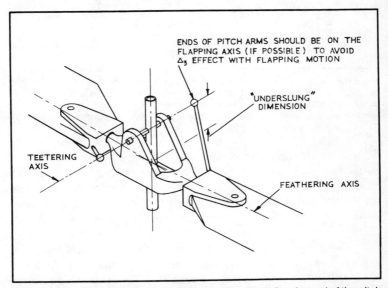

Fig. 8-11. Details of the underslung teetering rotor. Note that the end of the pitch arm must be on an extension of the teeter axis, or the blades will feather when they flap.

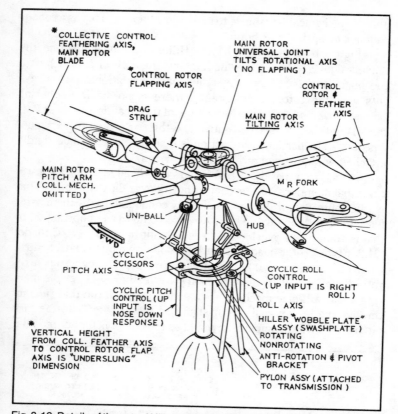

Fig. 8-12. Details of the actual Hiller rotor head. Note the control "paddles" (short airfoils) 90 degrees from the blades. Because of the universal joint at the top to which the main and control rotors are attached, the rotational axis tilts when a cyclic input is applied, so there is no flapping in a pure Hiller rotor (see Fig. 2-9). The pitch links are omitted for clarity.

So with the teetering rotor we usually make a choice between no collective and a servo rotor with 100 percent authority (as with many of the smaller models), or install collective control and settle for limited authority of the servo rotor by means of a mixing link as with some of the larger more sophisticated models as seen in Fig. 8-13.

There are two important features of the Hiller rotor head that are not generally incorporated in our R/C Hiller type rotors. I wonder how many people are aware that the "Hiller Rotomatic" system, as it was called, had a mechanical flapping feedback input to the control rotor which opposed main rotor flapping with a subsequent improvement in damping. Figure 8-14 shows the cyclic control concept. Figure 8-15 demonstrates how this flapping feedback signal works to reduce excessive main rotor flapping. The upper drawing in Fig. 8-15 is a stabilized hovering rotor. In the bottom drawing, the rotor has flapped to the left from a gust, or the rotor is flapping due to the short period oscillation described in Chapter 4. Notice that due to the "underslung" hub and the cyclic scissors, when the hub is thus flapped, the control rotor airfoils assume an angle of attack change that is in opposition to, and will reduce, excessive flapping during the next rotor revolution (see Fig. 5-5). This increased damping, of course, increases the time of the oscillation period which makes the machine easier to handle.

Then too, it didn't take the aerodynamic engineers very long to discover that the control rotor airfoil surfaces had to be set to a relatively high incidence angle (+9 on all "Rotomatic" heads after about 1949) or the machine could be subject to a condition of high

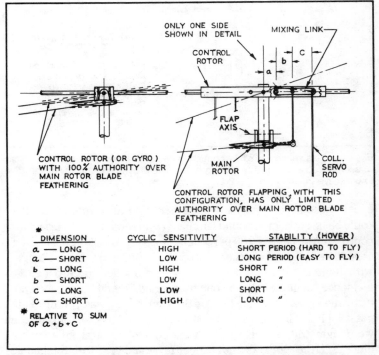

DIMENSION	CYCLIC SENSITIVITY	STABILITY (HOVER)
a — LONG	HIGH	SHORT PERIOD (HARD TO FLY)
a — SHORT	LOW	LONG PERIOD (EASY TO FLY)
b — LONG	HIGH	SHORT "
b — SHORT	LOW	LONG "
c — LONG	LOW	SHORT "
c — SHORT	HIGH	LONG "

* RELATIVE TO SUM OF *a* + *b* + *c*

Fig. 8-13. There is a trade-off between input control authority and stability with the conventional model teetering rotor. There are several variations of this concept.

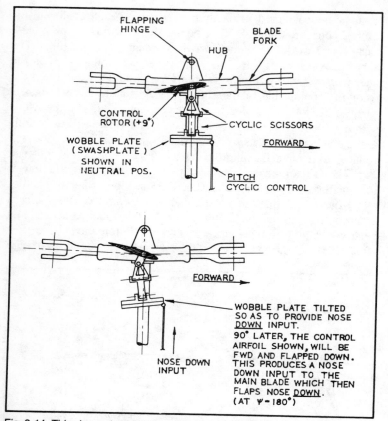

Fig. 8-14. This shows the cyclic control on an actual Hiller helicopter. The cyclic scissors act as a kind of filter. They are sensitive to cyclic inputs but not sensitive to collective inputs. See Fig. 8-2.

speed, nose slightly low, and in a steep right turn from which there could be no recovery. Sound familiar? (And remember, this is with a control rotor that has 100 percent authority!) At Lake Charles, La., several years ago, I watched four expertly flown .61 size JetRangers with limited authority control-rotor airfoils set to zero degrees incidence "auger in"—each one from a high-speed right-hand steep turn, and in each case the man on the transmitter was yelling "I ain't got it!" I later did a mathematical analysis* of this problem and then we demonstrated that, no, with the control rotor airfoils set to a high angle the model did not "auger in"—and yes, with the paddles

*See *R/C Modeler* magazine August 1977.

set to zero incidence, it did revert, instantly, into kit form (just as theory says it would).

Advantages of the teetering rotor-modified.

☐ The addition of a control rotor provides a certain amount of gyroscopic stabilization for gust control or oscillation. That is, it provides pitch and roll damping.

☐ The control rotor acts as a "servo booster" that provides cyclic inputs to the main rotor blades with very low input forces from the electronic servos.

☐ The system is relatively simple, lightweight, and low cost.

☐ This configuration, as modified, and in consideration of the present state of the art, is the best overall type for a novice to build and learn to fly.

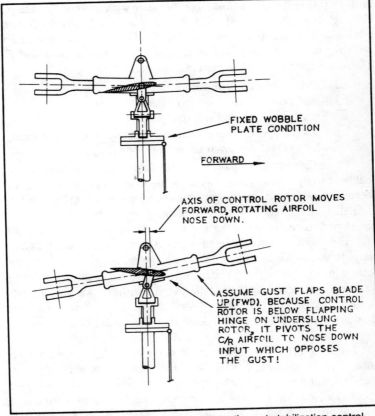

Fig. 8-15. The Hiller rotor head had an automatic gust stabilization control.

Disadvantages of the teetering rotor-modified

☐ Models having this configuration, although relatively easy to control, are nevertheless statically and dynamically unstable.

☐ Unless the teetering hinge is heavily snubbed (or damped) the control power and following rate are relatively poor.

☐ This configuration does not easily accommodate *both* collective control and 100 percent control rotor authority over the main rotor. The consequence (if collective is installed) is that there will be either a degradation of main rotor cyclic response, or short period oscillation dynamic instability.

THE RIGID ROTOR

The term *rigid rotor* is, of course a misnomer. Perhaps a better title would be *rigid hub rotor*, because with this configuration, although the hub is bolted solidy to the shaft, the *blades* do flex as pitch and roll moments are developed. The concept is discussed with regard to stability and controllability in Chapters 4 and 5. There we learned that, in general, the rigid rotor has:

☐ Tremendous control power.

☐ Rapid positive response to inputs.

☐ Very high pitch and roll damping.

☐ Positive speed stability, negative angle of attack stability which results in pitch-up with power chops.

From the above, we gather that the *basic* rigid rotor would be a real bear to fly unless some way could be found to tame it. To date, there have been two basic approaches to "domesticating" it, but I'm sure that as the state of the art progresses, other ideas will be developed to really bring the rigid rotor to its full potential.

The most commonly used method involves installing heavy weights in the blade tips. Thus, with the added tip weights, the rotor which is (almost) rigid becomes a large gyroscope to which the airframe is attached by the rotating shift. With the weights added, the rotor basic characteristics listed above are still present, but they are now subdued to the point that the model is more easily controllable.

This modification, however, is not a cure-all. There are two notable problems. First, with, say, three ounces of lead added to each tip (and this is about what it takes), the centrifugal force is just about doubled for the average rotor. Unless this is taken into account in the form of stronger hub components, a serious and disastrous failure may result. Second, because the rotor becomes a large gyro, a moment which may be imposed on it from a swinging airframe due to a sudden maneuver will cause a precession and an input to the rotor, usually about 70 degrees later. Once this begins, unless the man on the transmitter is very skillful, he will end up chasing the model around the lot in a slow, circular, drifting oscillation while holding constant heading. Control is difficult, because a pure input will result in a bias response, and after two or three corrections, the modeler becomes disoriented as to how to make the next corrective input.

Advantages of the rigid rotor with tip weights.

☐ No lead-lag or flapping hinges required.

☐ Because of heavy tip weights, built-in-coning can be neglected (i.e., blades straight across).

☐ Control system is very simple.

☐ Very high control-power which permits large CG range and/or higher maneuverability.

☐ This configuration is adaptable to any number of blades. It should be noted that although two-bladed rigid motors are quite successful, vibration during a pitch or roll will be high because, of course, twice-per-revolution, the two-bladed rotor is incapable of generating a control moment, whereas, a three or four-bladed rigid rotor can generate an almost constant moment regardless of blade position.

Disadvantages of the rigid rotor with tip weights.

☐ The added tip weights cause very high centrifugal force (about twice normal) and the affected structure must be designed and built to safely carry this added load.

☐ Servo wear and battery drain will be higher than normal because the blade feathering forces that the servos are exposed to are several times higher than those that operate control rotor feathering.

☐ This configuration has a tendency toward a circular pattern hover instability similar to the hover oscillation of the teetering rotor discussed in the section on stability. With the rigid rotor, a corrective input introduces a cross-coupling bias response that tends to aggravate the circular drift which further degrades the oscillation, whereas with the teetering rotor, all corrections are simply made *against* the undesired direction of motion.

☐ Because the phase angle (ϕ) of the rigid rotor is considerably less than 90 degrees (usually about 70 for R/C models),

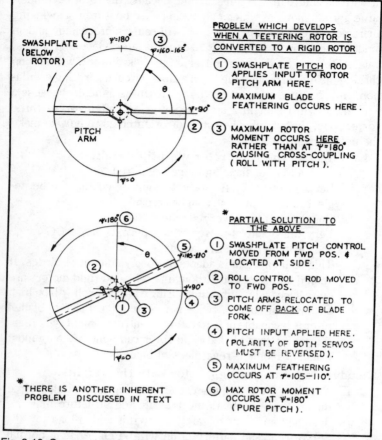

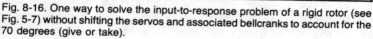

Fig. 8-16. One way to solve the input-to-response problem of a rigid rotor (see Fig. 5-7) without shifting the servos and associated bellcranks to account for the 70 degrees (give or take).

the maximum blade feathering must occur about 70 degrees before the desired point of maximum moment. This can be done as shown in Fig. 8-16.

It was noted earlier that, to date, two approaches to the rigid rotor had been tried. The tip weights is one way. The other way to tame the rigid rotor is by means of a rate gyro having 100 percent authority over it. This was the classic approach used by Lockheed on the Model 286 which completed the world's first round loops and true slow rolls back in 1967. This same system was used on the Lockheed Cheyenne. To my knowledge there has been only one

R/C model helicopter* ever built using the actual Lockheed control system concept. I say *concept* because all the elements were present as in the full size counterpart except that the model servos were electrically driven, whereas the full size servos, of course, were driven by hydraulic pressure.

In Chapter 4 it was noted this was the only configuration to the author's knowledge to have positive static and dynamic stability. Although the system is quite complex and is, therefore, probably beyond the feasibility of ever being kitted, perhaps giving you some fresh ideas, a description of the control system concept is included here. Figure 8-17 is a schematic of the mechanics of the cyclic control.

---

*Other than development model Lockheed flown around 1959-1960.

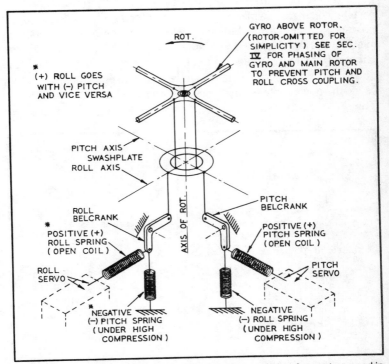

Fig .8-17. The classic rigid rotor, 100% authority gyro and spring system used in the author's Lockheed Cheyenne. The general concept is similar to that of the full-size machine except the full-size machine used hydraulic prime movers instead of electrically driven servos. A French company also used this concept in their four-blade rigid rotor.

The essence of the system is that the pitch and roll bellcranks are each highly loaded by a compressive (−) spring on the bellcrank at dead center. The other arm of each bellcrank is connected to a servo actuator (pitch or roll) by means of an open-wound coil positive (+) spring. Spring forces and mechanical dimensions are such that, with the servo at neutral, the bellcrank can be rotated either to stretch or compress the (+) spring and there would be no net load on the bellcrank; it will remain at rest in any position. Figure 8-18 reveals how this comes about. The highly compressed (−) spring force times the offset distance, as the bellcrank rotates, must always equal the spring force times its offset distance (from the bellcrank center).

First of all, the reason that there must be no force on the bellcrank when the gyro displaces after precessing is that for the gyro to have pure precession (90 degrees), the gyro must feel *no* resistance to the displacement. Let's refer to Fig. 8-19, apply a nose-down input from the cyclic lever, and see how this control system works. A nose-down signal rotates the pitch servo arm (right side of figure). This lengthens the pitch (+) spring, creating a down force at the swashplate. There is no displacement here because the down force is acting on a free gyro which resists the force. The gyro subsequently responds by precessing (or displacing)

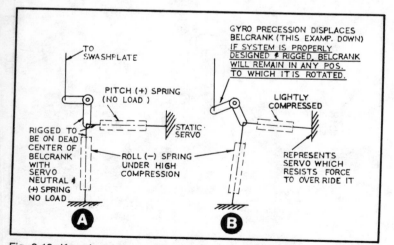

Fig. 8-18. Key element on which the system is based. The author had two problems with the system which were never completely overcome: 1) system rigidity without a big weight penalty. 2) At the time it was built 1974-1977, no small but sufficiently powerful servos were commercially available to provide crisp response. Stability was the best, to date, of any model helicopter.

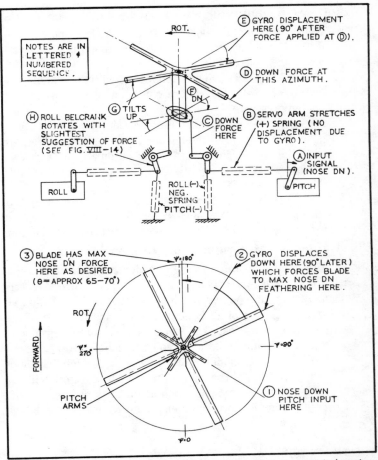

Fig. 8-19. This diagram shows how the author's Cheyenne control system worked. Follow the notes in numbered sequence.

downward 90 degrees, or a quarter of a revolution, later. The gyro so precesses because it, as we noted earlier, meets no resistance on the other axis (at the roll positive spring). Because the gyro, by definition, has 100 percent authority over the blades, there is hard linkage from each gyro arm to a blade and consequently the blades feather as the gyro tilts.

As noted in Fig. 8-19, with this configuration, great care must be taken, where around the azimuth, the gyro receives the *force* signal so that the maximum blade *moment* will be achieved at the desired azimuth so as to preclude cross-coupling.

Advantages of rigid rotor with gyro.

☐ Neutral or slightly positive static stability and positive dynamic stability in hover and in forward flight (best stability of any type to date).

☐ This R/C model configuration moves with the smoothness and grace of the full size machines instead of like a cork bobbing on water.

☐ A throttle chop in forward flight results in no perceptable nose-up pitch due to the absolute control of the free gyro over the rotor. That is, the gyro automatically applies a corrective input so rapidly the pitch-up never has time to develop.

☐ The four-blade rigid rotor is, in general, more capable of autorotation than two-blade rotors because the four blades have a greater driving force to overcome drivetrain friction.

Disadvantages of the rigid rotor with gyro.

☐ The control system is very complex and difficult to rig.

☐ The design of the cyclic control system is critical. All parts including the power of the servos, positive/negative springs, length of all bellcrank arms, and the size of the gyro must be selected and/or designed as an integral system. For example, if the servos or the positive springs are too weak, the model is extremely stable but has poor controllability. If the gyro is too small, controllability is adequate, but static and dynamic stability are degraded.

☐ This system is not recommended for rotors with less than three blades.

THE TAIL ROTOR

There are several points to be emphasized on R/C model helicopter tail rotors (Fig. 8-20). For one thing, they tend to be designed undersized. On a calm day in hover, the blades operate at a very high lift coefficient—so high, in fact, that a sudden yaw input against main rotor torque will sometimes stall the tail rotor, and the machine will yaw in the opposite direction (with torque). An increase in rotor diameter of about 10 percent will make quite a difference in models having the above tendency. The skittish yaw tendency will usually be alleviated.

Another subject which always starts discussion is what airfoil section to use—flat bottomed? Symmetrical? I know of one full-size machine that used an undercambered section like a thin RAF-32.

Fig. 8-20. A typical tail rotor. The main rotor on this model turned counterclockwise (looking down). The tail rotor, therefore, is on the correct side of the tail boom for a counterclockwise main rotor.

Would you believe another type used *flat* blades? They were about 9 percent thickness with a blunted, slightly cambered leading edge and a wedge for a trailing edge. Because of the small size of model blades and their low operating Reynolds Number, their airfoil shape probably doesn't affect the performance very much. They should have a smooth surface (if for no other reason than looks!), not too blunt a leading edge, and a sharp trailing edge.

Then there was a briefly fashionable trend awhile back—the teetering tail rotor with a "delta three" (Δ_3) flapping hinge. This is used almost universally on full size helicopters, but it is of no value on models. Let's see why it is used at all, and then we can see why it contributes nothing to the R/C helicopter. In the early development of the full size machines, tail rotors had rigid hubs, and they had frequent shaft fatigue failures (which invariably ruined an entire afternoon). Why the failures? Well, it's the same old inherent rotor characteristic we found in Chapter 2 where a thrusting rotor, advancing edgewise into the wind, will always try to flap back so that the thrust vector is pointing away from the advancing air, remember? Figure 8-21 is a top view of an advancing helicopter showing the direction of rotation of the main rotor and the consequent direction of thrust of the tail rotor to overcome main rotor torque.

With the tail rotor thrust to the right, the blades will try to flap

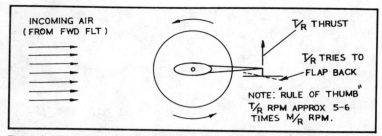

Fig. 8-21. This figure supplements the text on why teetering tail rotors are required on full-size machines but *not* on any models.

as shown by the dotted line, which subjects the rotating shaft to high alternating bending loads and hence sometimes fatigue failure. To prevent bending fatigue in the tail rotor shaft, the tail rotors were designed to teeter. This alleviated the shaft bending, but now the tail rotor shaft had to be lengthened to avoid the blades making contact with the tail boom. Furthermore, as the rotor flaps, i.e., as the tail *rotor* angle of attack increases, the thrust to the right increases. This results in a need for almost constant corrective yaw inputs in forward flight which leads to erratic directional control.

The simple solution to the problem was to skew the teeter axis around as shown in Fig. 8-22. When the teeter axis is so inclined, it is apparent that as blade (A) flaps into the paper, the angle of attack automatically increases (due to the angle) and similarly as blade (B) flaps out of the paper the angle of attack decreases so as to oppose the excessive flapping. This tilted teetering axis is referred to as "Δ_3 action." Now, the full-size machines could use short tail rotor shafts with Δ_3 action, and the shaft is not exposed to excessive

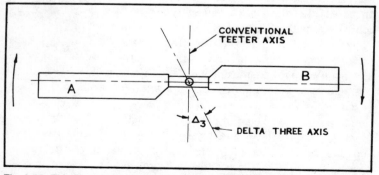

Fig. 8-22. This figure supplements the text on the little understood "Δ_3" concept as to why it is almost always used on full-size machines but does absolutely nothing for our models.

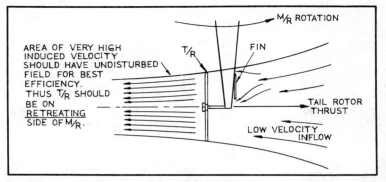

Fig. 8-23. A study on which side of the fuselage the tail rotor should be placed when designing a scratchbuilt machine.

loads. The rotor teetering is all but eliminated and the erratic yawing tendency (sometimes called wandering) due to the straight teetering blade is gone. Back to R/C models. We have seen from the above discussion why Δ_3 is important to full-size machines, but our R/C model tail rotor shafts are many times stronger than if they were built to absolute scale. The model tail rotor shafts, therefore, are seldom if ever subject to failure from *air loads* (we're not talking ground impact here), and thus there is no justification for a teetering and Δ_3 hinge on an R/C model tail rotor.

The bottom line: You may hear marvelous claims for a Δ_3 teetering rotor on R/C models, don't get all upset if your models do not have it—you aren't missing anything!

In general, the tail rotor should be located on the retreating side of the main rotor as shown in Fig. 8-23. The tail rotor so positioned is more efficient than if it were positioned on the other side because the high velocity air (the air downstream from the tail rotor) is unobstructed in its flow, whereas if the high velocity air (downstream) impinged on the closely located fuselage, fin, etc., the blades are more susceptable to stall due to turbulence from the impingement.

Rotation either way is okay for all R/C model tail rotors. In a full-size machine, direction can be critical from the standpoint of aerodynamic interference and also from the standpoint of picking up rocks, debris, etc., and slinging it into the main rotor blades, causing damage. R/C models, however, have much lower main rotor induced velocities than their full-size counterparts. Thus, aerodynamic interference and FOD (foreign object damage) to the blades is not a serious problem.

Chapter 9

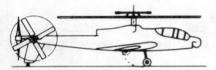

Helpful Design Hints for a Scratchbuilt

You would be well-advised *not* to make your first R/C helicopter a scratchbuilt. You should have some experience and understanding of mechanical principles, access to some machine tools (small lathe, drill press with vice, band saw with metal-cutting blade, grinder, and assorted drills, taps, and dies). Last, and equally important, would be a buddy in your vicinity who has built one. If you can manage the above, then by all means go to it! If you persevere, the rewards will be great. The accomplishment you will feel will far overshadow all the nitty-gritty problems that inevitably loom to be solved (Fig. 9-1).

How do you go about it? Well, the first decision concerns the general size of the helicopter to be built (Fig. 9-2). This may be decided for you by the kind of engine that is available or that you wish to use. Also at this point, a decision should be forthcoming on the degree of sophistication you have in mind—a simple bolt-together trainer, an aerobatic type, or perhaps a "standoff scale" with fiberglass fuselage, etc. This decision will to some extent be influenced by your available shop facilities and also by the number of radio channels available to you. Don't rush into things at this stage. Take several weeks to think through the pros and cons of each decision. Even the simplest "bolt-together" should have about two to three weeks (evenings and weekends) of casual thought during this stage. ("Scratchbuilt" as used here, incidentally, means that most parts are designed by you and built specifically for this new

Fig. 9-1. The author's scratchbuilt Lockheed AH-56A Cheyenne.

machine, as compared to lifting out the "mechanics" from one airframe and installing in another.)

A sketching pad 8½×11 inches with ¼×¼ inch light grid lines with three-ring binder holes and a binder are useful. Freehand sketches (with any erasures) are made of various arrangements including engine location and position, clutch, gears, belts, tail rotor takeoff point, main rotor shaft location, direction of rotation, and numerous other items as they come up. After a few weeks of

Fig. 9-2. A .40 size four-bladed rigid rotor. Note tapered blades.

this madness you will begin to have a collection of sketches in your design note book that "sorta" define what you think you are trying to do.

At this point it is a good idea to stop sketching arrangements and "firm up" several major design parameters including rotor diameter, blade chord, rotor RPM, fuselage length (usually heavily influenced by the rotor diameter), and a first estimate of the weight of the proposed machine. The obvious question here is, of course, "How can I determine the weight of something that hasn't been designed yet?" Well, the engine and airborne electronics can be weighed or the numbers obtained from the manufacturers' specifications. As for the drive train, rotor head, blades, tail rotor, fuselage, and landing gear, an educated guess based on past experience or the weight of on-hand similar parts is good enough for the present. Sometimes another modeler may have clutches, gears, etc., not too unlike what you have in mind that can be weighed.

Now armed with a proposed engine size and a first estimate of gross weight of the proposed model, you are ready to retire to Appendix B to systematically determine main rotor diameter, blade chord, and RPM, and then go one step further and reassure yourself that the proposed machine will not require more power than your engine can produce. If it appears, for example, from the rapid calculation of power in Appendix B that the power available will be marginal, your options of course are to go to a more powerful engine, reduce the disc loading (larger diameter rotor or find a way to reduce the weight), and/or reduce the rotor solidity (again increase the rotor diameter but keep the same chord). Reducing main rotor RPM will also reduce the power required (less profile power loss), but the main rotor will operate at a higher lift coefficient (higher than best lift/drag). This means a higher operating torque, and consequently, a larger tail rotor and/or higher tail rotor RPM will be required—which defeats the purpose, so this option should be only the *last* resort.

After the above exercises have been completed and it looks as though you have a design rotor diameter, chord, RPM, and tail rotor diameter and RPM, the next step is to make a full size layout of the entire helicopter on shelf paper or whatever. It helps if you have a drawing board and T square, but these aren't absolutely necessary. This layout will consist in general of very fine, accurately drawn construction lines that locate most of the components and define the space envelope that is allotted to each item. This layout will include such detail as establishing a reference datum line from which all components and subcomponents are accurately located and positioned, including engine, main rotor, tail rotor, tail rotor drive, and tail rotor shaft centerlines. Use the actual engine to measure and lay out its position, as well as those of clutches, gears, belts, etc. There will be many backtracks and erasures, and at times you will even go back to the sketching pad to explore other arrangements. This is all part of the picture; don't become discouraged. I guarantee the end result is worth some suffering here. Also, as you progress through this stage, start a weight-and-balance table (covered later in this chapter). One more comment on the layout: Keep in mind that the objective of the layout is to give you an accurate picture of the relative location, position, and space envelope for each assembly, subassembly, and component, and also the interface of the various subassemblies.

The final stage is to make working drawings of each part, using the layout as a guide, and dimension each drawing so that the part can be fabricated from the drawing. As you proceed, check stress levels as shown in Appendix C. It is also helpful here, with the more complicated parts, to study your finished working drawings and then write up what I call a "machining sequence" which is a chronological order of machine operations. For example, on a main rotor blade fork, you would probably block out a rectangular blank from aluminum plate. Mount it on the lathe first and drill and bore accurately, then saw out the curved profile, etc. If the reverse procedure is used, it might be difficult to mount the part in the lathe or to accurately locate the bore axis for the bearings. Complete all of the above (with one exception as noted in determining rotor teeter height later in this chapter) before cutting any material because you may have to backtrack on your design somewhere along the line. If you have already cut material affected by the change in design, then the cut material might be rendered unusable. You will end up with a design notebook containing the sketches, calculations, and working drawings that will completely define the machine you are about to build.

A simple, conventional bolt-together machine will require probably about 20 to 30 pages to completely define. By comparison, my scratchbuilt Lockheed Cheyenne (Fig. 9-3), designed and built in 1974-75 (which had the four-bladed rigid rotor, authentic cyclic control concept, collective pitch, R/C controllable pitch three-bladed pusher propeller, four-bladed tail rotor off the end of the stabilizer, wings, and a specially designed retractable landing gear,) required about a year of design work and a notebook that has about

Fig. 9-3. The Lockheed Cheyenne in a high-speed pass. Note the rotor is level. The forward thrust is provided by the pusher propeller at the tail end, as seen through the tail rotor disc.

150 pages. Even then, the inevitable happened. On several occasions I found that I had designed something that was impossible to build—so it was back to the drawing board! Sound familar?

Table 9-1 should help the scratchbuilder in his approach to the rotor design. The values listed are not "cast in concrete," but are representative of average design parameters that can be expected to give reasonably good results. They can be leaned a little either way without creating a catastrophe.

Figure 9-4 reveals why an aerobatic R/C helicopter is better with four blades than with two. Although two-bladed rotors are capable of aerobatics, and even sustained inverted flight, it is obvious from Fig. 9-4 that the rolling (or pitching) moment follows what is called a *sinusoidal function* and, for a roll, when the blades are at azimuth of (0) and 180 degrees, i.e., twice per revolution, the *moment is zero*. Figure 9-5 compares the rolling (or pitching) moments that are capable of being generated with a two-bladed versus a four-bladed rotor.

THE UNDERSLUNG TEETERING HUB

Chapter 8 contains a discussion on why the underslung hub is a great advantage because it reduces vibration when a teetering rotor flaps. Let's see how we would go about determining how much to raise the teeter axis.

Table 9-2. Rotor Design Guidelines.

Mission	Rotor Type	Number of Blades	Disc Loading Lbs/ft	Solidity ▽	Mean Lift Coefficient $\bar{c}_L$	Suggested Engine Size In³ Displ.	Target Gross Weight Lbs.
Trainer	"Hiller" Type	2	.40	.045	.45	.40	6
High Payload (mostly hover)	"Hiller" Type	2	.30	.035	.80	.61	15
High Speed	Rigid	3 or 4	.65	.07	.28	.61	9
Aerobatic	Rigid	3 or 4	.70	.10	.25	.61	8¾

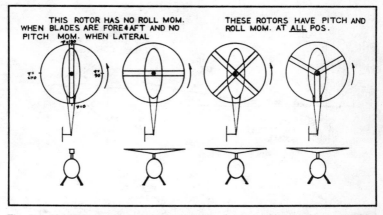

Fig. 9-4. Moment generating characteristics of rotors with two, three, and four blades.

Once the rotor diameter chord, RPM, and a first estimate of weight are all calculated, determine the coning angle by the method in Chapter 1. Rotor coning has two important functions: 1) The obvious one is to relieve the large bending moment at the hub by "building in" the correct amount of deflection created when the lift and centrifugal moments are in equilibrium; and 2) to maintain the blade axis as closely as possible to the feathering axis. The importance of this second function is best illustrated in Fig. 9-6.

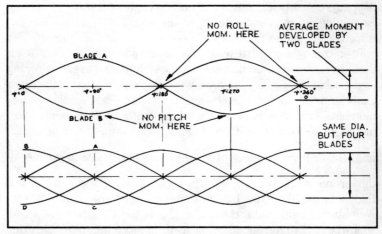

Fig. 9-5. These curves show the total pitch or roll moment at any given instant, and the approximate average of the moments available, for a two and a four-bladed rotor.

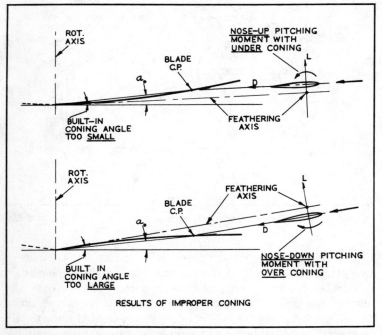

RESULTS OF IMPROPER CONING

Fig. 9-6. With reference to Fig. 1-5, the twisting motion imposed on a blade that is under-coned or over-coned is shown.

The root of the problem is that with all except individually flapping rotor blades, the actual coning angle of a blade is seldom exactly at the built-in angle. It varies with RPM, model weight, rotor thrust, and in forward flight—even around the azimuth. The built-in coning angle that we calculate and put into the rotor head, then, is targeted to be as close as possible to the average coning angle—that is, at which the rotor will be operating most of the time. Built-in rotor coning thereby minimizes excessive hub bending moments and also undesirable blade feathering moments. Remember, we found that if the blade is, say, for a .40 size or under, and is made from *one* piece of wood, you are pretty safe to use the $\dfrac{R}{\sqrt{3}}$ dimension in determining the CF. If the blade is larger and/or you find after building the blades that you must use mass balance weights to position the chordwise CG at the CP, then the *actual* spanwise CG (determined by balance) is more accurate. This discussion implies, incidentally, that you will save yourself time and extra work if you build the blades *before* "fixing" the one final dimension of how high the teeter axis should be raised. (This is the one exception mentioned earlier.)

Now, using a protractor lay out the full-size center lines representing the mast and the blades as illustrated in Fig. 9-7. Measure from the shaft centerline out each blade a distance $\frac{R}{\sqrt{3}}$ where $\sqrt{3} = 1.73$ or the actual determined CG if mass balance weights are added. Connect the two points on the blade by a straight line horizontally across. Now measure the dimension from where the shaft axis intersects the two blade centerlines up to the horizontal line connecting the blade CG. This measured dimension is, then, the amount the teeter is raised above the blades. Complete this detail of the teetering hub drawing and you are on your way!

MAKING MAIN ROTOR BLADES

Each time I have noticed the list price for prefabricated rotor blades, the urgent need for this section became more evident. Main rotor blades for small helicopters (.40 size and under) are usually made from a single piece of wood. I have found that *clear* white fir or white pine are two of several woods that work well for these smaller blades. It is usually convenient to make a half a dozen or more at a time. (That is, if you fly as I do!) Select the most efficient arrange-

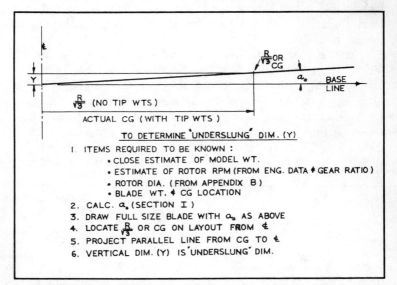

Fig. 9-7. In designing your scratchbuilt rotor, this is the procedure used to determine the "underslung" dimension (see Figs. 8-10, 8-11).

Fig. 9-8. Getting the greatest number of blades from a dressed "2 by 4 inch" plank.

ment so as to obtain the greatest number of blades from the selected piece of new stock. For example, if the raw stock is a dressed 2×4 inches and the blade chord is to be 1½ inches, the logical layout would look something like Fig. 9-8.

Thickness (T) of each sawn slab should be about 1/32 inch thicker than the planned finished airfoil if you are using a fine-toothed band saw, or about 1/16 inch thicker if the local lumber company makes the slab cuts because their saws very often make rougher cuts. The standard dressed 1×2 inch piece also provides a convenient arrangement, as shown in Fig. 9-9.

This will yield about three blades per length, so that a 1×2 inch finished piece twice as long as the blade intended length should yield three sets. When selecting the lumber, pick straight stock, clear, and grain matched as nearly as possible (this will pay off later when balancing the rotor). Some *minor* grain irregularities can be tolerated as shown in Fig. 9-10.

The next step is to dress the blade blanks down to the desired length, chord, and thickness. One handy and rapid way to do this involves a drill press and a 2½ to 3 inch diameter sanding drum (the larger the better for this operation) obtainable in any good hardware store. A simple but fairly accurate sanding guide can be made, as shown in Fig. 9-11, from a piece of 2×6 inch scrap about 12-14 inches long. The 2×6 piece has a round hole sawn near one edge as shown. The diameter of the hole should be about one half inch

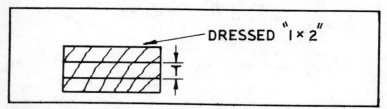

Fig. 9-9. For the smaller models (.40 size engine) a "1 by 2 inch" is a convenient size to use as shown.

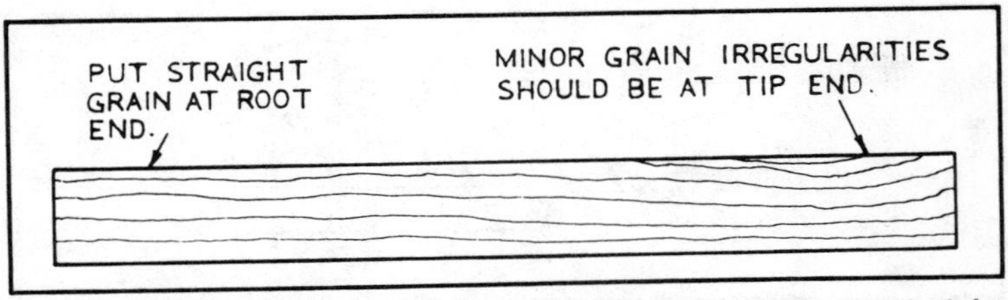

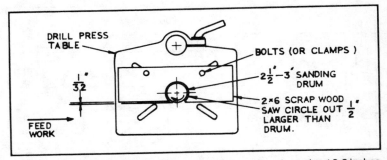

Fig. 9-10. In selecting wood for a blade, whether single or two-piece, look for straight grain. Small "waves" or variations can be tolerated. Place that end at the tip. Stay away from any wood that is near a knot.

greater than your sanding drum. Notice in Fig. 9-11 the direction of rotation of the drill press (conventional) and that the edges of the 2×6 on either side of the hole are true and smooth with the work always moving from left to right. Notice also that the left side surface (the "feed" side) is made so that it sets back about 1/32 inch, *no more*. Thus, when the 2×6 guide is clamped to the drill press table with the drum tangent to the right-hand surface, and the work is held firmly against both left and right guide surfaces as it is moved, an accurate, smoothly sanded surface will result. Successive passes will reduce the thickness of the work as desired.

When larger rotor blades are involved (that is, for the .61 size engines), it is advisable to go to the two-piece blade in order to maintain the proper mass balance (chordwise) without having to add an excessive amount of weight to the leading edge (see Chapter 1). Straight-grained white oak for the leading edge and balsa for the trailing edge is one good combination. The hardwood leading edge should constitute about 33 percent of the chord. For example, let's assume the chord to be 2.25 inches with a thickness of 15 percent. This means the hardwood leading edge spar dimension should be

Fig. 9-11. If you have access to a drill press and a sanding drum about 2-3 inches in diameter, you can make an excellent sander by cutting a scrap piece of 2×6 inch plank about one foot long as shown. Note the 1/32" recess on the *feed* side.

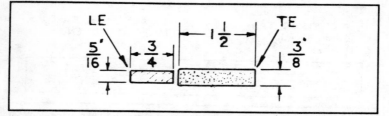

Fig. 9-12. End view of the two pieces of a composite blade. Note that the trailing edge (TE) is thicker than the hardwood leading edge (LE). After bonding, the soft balsa TE can be sanded to the same thickness as the LE.

approximately 5/16 × ¾ inches. Incidentally, note that unlike a wing in which the spar is positioned vertically to provide resistance to bending up and down, the rotor blade spar is far stronger for its size because it must withstand very high tension (CF). It is this centrifugal force that prevents the blade from bending very far up and down, and so it is laid flat to permit the thin airfoil section.

Back to the blade construction—if the hardwood spar is to be 5/16 × ¾, then the balsa trailing edge should be ⅜ × 1½ inches. The reason for the thicker balsa trailing edge is to facilitate easier matching of the edges when they are pinned together. Figure 9-12 shows how these two blanks will match before the final dressing down. The matching surfaces should be sanded carefully to remove any high spots so that little or no light shows through when the pieces are pressed together by hand. I prefer to key the two pieces together with dowel pins with about 5 or 6 inch spacing. These pins not only stabilize the joint while the glue is setting, but they also contribute to a stronger finished blade. Figure 9-13 reveals the details.

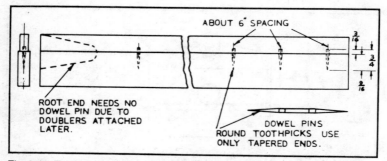

Fig. 9-13. To assist while bonding and to add strength to the finished blade, use dowels every six inches or so. I use round toothpicks as shown. The root end needs no dowel because they will be reinforced with doublers on both sides.

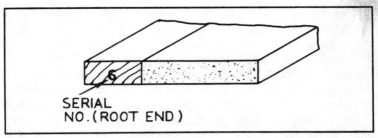

SERIAL
NO.(ROOT END)

Fig. 9-14. The finished two-piece blade blank.

At this point the blades should be serialized by using an ink marking pen at the root end of the leading and trailing edges to be joined (Fig. 9-14). Now mark the location of the holes for the dowels on the edge of the hardwood, then match the trailing edge by laying it alongside and mark the corresponding holes in the balsa. Clamp a piece of scrap wood with a straight edge to the drill press table so that the dowel drill will enter the hardwood edge to be bonded midway between the upper and lower surfaces. The hole in the hardwood should be the same diameter as the dowel and about 3/16 to ¼ inch deep (no deeper, to avoid weakening the spar). If the drill press is so equipped, use the depthstop to assure all holes are the same and be certain to hold the spar against the guide so that each hole is centered. Repeat the above with the trailing edge. Remember to relocate the clamped straight edge because the balsa trailing edge is a little thicker, and the depth stop will also be readjusted to take the full depth of the dowel pin.

When this is complete, try fitting the mating surfaces together with the dowel pins in place for a dry run (Fig. 9-15). Next cut some

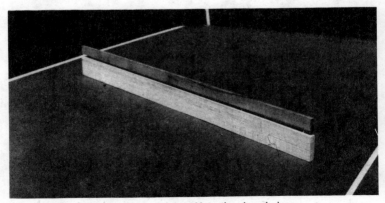

Fig. 9-15. Blade blanks before joining. Note the dowel pins.

scrap wood pieces about ¼ × ½ × 8 or 10 inches long. These pieces will fit between the blade components and the clamps to prevent clamp marks on the blade. When all is ready call your wife or girlfriend (this will really make brownie points with her)! Coat all surfaces to be bonded, including holes and dowels, with aliphatic resin, insert the dowels in the hardwood, match the holes in the balsa trailing edge, and press together. Have your helper position the clamping sticks along the full length of the leading and trailing edges while you apply C clamps every 4 to 5 inches (Fig. 9-16). The clamps should be pulled up just tight enough to close the joint and force little beads of resin out along the joint. Any further tightening of the clamps may crush the balsa or put a camber in the assembly. Be sure the balsa extends beyond the hardwood both sides full length. The clamps should stay on for at least six to eight hours (longer if convenient). A dozen clamps will usually handle two blades at a time. You can be working the first set after the resin is hard, while the second pair are in the clamps, etc.

You should now have a half a dozen or so of blade blanks in which the balsa is thicker than the hardwood leading edge. Using the sanding setup in Fig. 9-11, make repeated light passes to dress down the balsa trailing edge block to the same thickness as the hardwood leading edge as shown in Fig. 9-14. Don't despair if you goof and sand the softer balsa below the hardwood (or find it didn't come up to the edge of the hardwood in the first place). Merely glue on a piece of 1/32 or 1/16 inch sheet balsa to more than cover the problem, then resand to match the hardwood.

Fig. 9-16. The blank components are held in place by clamps until the aliphatic resin hardens. Notice the protective strips between the blade and the clamps.

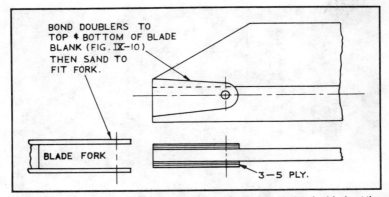

Fig. 9-17. Details of how the doublers are located and bonded to the blade at the root (attachment) end.

Generally, the larger two-piece rotor blades have root doublers that are bonded to the blank at this stage of construction. These reinforcement pieces are cut from three (or preferably five) ply birch plywood obtainable at any hobby shop. The thickness should be selected such that when the doublers are cemented on the top and bottom of the blade root as shown in Fig. 9-17, the total thickness of blade blank plus doublers is slightly thicker than the inside dimension of the movable hub or *blade fork* as it is usually called. After the aliphatic resin has hardened, use a sanding block and paper to obtain an easy slip fit of the blade doublers into the fork.

At this point you should make a metal contour of the airfoil. It can be either aluminum or brass sheet metal, and can be just half a contour if the section is symmetrical or only the top surface if the airfoil is flat on the bottom. It should be a smooth contour with no irregularities. Hold it against the ends and trace the airfoil with a ballpoint pen as shown in Fig. 9-18. Now using the ballpoint pen and your fingers to provide the proper spacing, block out the blade blank

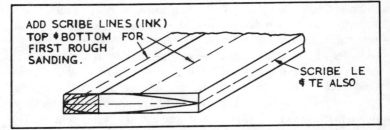

Fig. 9-18. The blade blank is blocked as shown to serve as rough sanding guides.

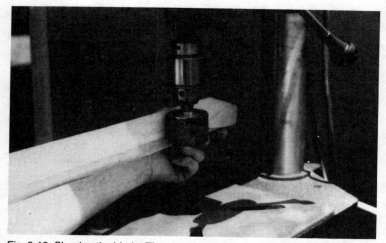

Fig. 9-19. Shaping the blade. The trick is to always keep the blade moving. You will be surprised how easy it is to shape the blade this way.

as shown in the figure using the end contours as guides for locating the blocking-out lines.

The next step is to make rough cuts using a coarse grit sanding drum down to the rough guidelines top and bottom. Use goggles and a painting mask whenever sanding. Start by taking off light cuts and always keep the blade moving—repeat, *always* moving back and forth (Fig. 9-19). You will be pleasantly surprised at how quickly you will be able to "arrive" at the roughed-out airfoil. As you move the root end of the blade near the sanding drum, use a little care so that the doublers are not sanded by mistake. A little ingenuity and I think you will soon be working right up to the doublers with no trouble. The blade at this point should still have some sharp corners at the leading edge, top and bottom, and a trailing edge that is now about 3/32 of an inch thick.

Now replace the coarse grit paper with finer grit on the sanding drum and begin to round off all sharp corners, sharpen the trailing edge to about 1/16 maximum, and blend the surface block lines out, top and bottom. As you sand from here on, occasionally hold the blade up edgewise to a light to reveal the irregularities which can be removed by the drum. Final sanding is accomplished with a hand-held block. Starting with about 100 grit, progress down to about 400 grit paper. During these final steps, frequent checks with the sheet metal master contour will reveal where any high spots remain. The trailing edge should be fairly straight and a maximum of 1/32 inch

Fig. 9-20. The finished two-piece blade showing the hardwood leading edge and the balsa trailing edge.

thick after the final sanding (Fig. 9-20).

The blade root attachment holes are drilled at this point. Several good ways of attaching the blade to the hub have been developed. Although .60 size models have been flown successfully with no in-plane restraint (that is, the blades are free to seek their own equilibrium lead-lag position), I feel that this is a very unwise practice unless you really know what you are doing. In high speed

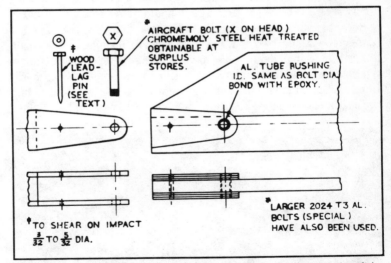

Fig. 9-21. (See Fig. 9-17.) Details of the blade attachment. A steel aircraft (or larger aluminum) bolt carries the centrifugal force. The wooden lead-lag pin keeps the blade in alignment, yet if it strikes something the wood pin will shear, minimizing damage. I *do not advise* flying the rotor with floating lead-lag freedom. The blade may get into in-plane resonance due to high speed and cyclic pitch.

forward flight, where the blade lift and drag distribution drastically shifts spanwise once each revolution, the blade may get into a resonant in-plane oscillation. These oscillations can have excursions of either lead or lag so great that serious pitching moments will result. This occurs when the blade center of pressure strays too far ahead or behind the feather axis. I favor the blade attachment shown in Fig. 9-21.

If you are making replacement blades for a kit model, then you should stay with the existing design. It obviously works well, so why change? But if you are designing your own model, you may wish to consider this method. The larger outboard hole carries all of the centrifugal force by means of a steel bolt or aluminum shear pin. The smaller inboard hole maintains lead-lag alignment by means of a wood dowel shear pin. This wood shear pin will shear off at first contact with anything (I have never had one fail or come out in flight). A drill jig is made up from scrap wood and a piece of one-quarter inch steel plate to serve as the drill guide, so that, as seen in Fig. 9-22, when each blade is held in place and drilled, the blades all come out with identical hole locations. As Fig. 9-21 indicates, the wood shear pins can be made from 3/32 inch wood dowel for .40 size models or from 5/32 or 3/16 wood dowel from a hobby shop for larger rotors. They should be made approximately one-fourth inch longer than the hub thickness and slightly tapered or rounded on the bottom end. For the heads, drill slightly undersized holes in 1/16 inch model plywood about one-half inch apart. Insert the dowels in the holes and bond with aliphatic resin. When hard, run a saw down between the rows of dowels and finish by rounding the heads against a sanding drum and you now have what looks like a

Fig. 9-22. A typical drill jig for blade attachment holes.

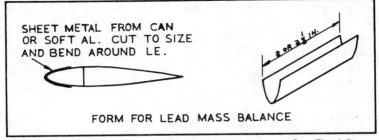

SHEET METAL FROM CAN
OR SOFT AL. CUT TO SIZE
AND BEND AROUND LE.

2 OR 2½ IN.

FORM FOR LEAD MASS BALANCE

Fig. 9-23. Details of making a lead mold for mass balance. See Fig. 1-9.

bunch of wooden nails! These dowel pins should have a snug fit, and as such, the blades will always have the same lead-lag position and consequently the rotor will remain in good chordwise balance. To remove the pins so as to fold the blades for storage, press up on the bottom with the thumbnail and the pins should come out.

At this point it is wise to determine the exact center of gravity of the blade using the method shown in Chapter 1. If the CG is no more than 25 percent back from the leading edge, you are ready to finish the blade. Most builders after final fine sanding remove all dust and then cover the blades with any of several pressure sensitive plastic films available. An alternate method involves polyester resin mixed with filler and then sanded progressively with finer grit paper until the surface is smooth with no grain marks showing. A final coat of color epoxy can then be applied to complete the blades.

TIP WEIGHTS

We discussed in Chapter 1 how to determine the amount of weight needed. Lead is ideal for this because it is easily worked and readily available from any tire shop. Cut a strip of soft aluminum about ¾×2 or 2½ inches long. If soft aluminum is not available, heat-treated aluminum can be annealed by holding it over a gas range fire and then allowed to cool slowly. (If still not soft, reheat to a higher temperature.) Sheet steel from a food can is easily worked but the lead may tend to stick to the can. Bend the metal around the blade leading edge as shown in Fig. 9-23. Now position it as a trough and seal both ends. The easiest way is to place two pieces of plywood over the ends and hold them in place with a C clamp. Bend a little "pour-spout" or lip into the edge of a can (unless you have an iron label) in which the junk lead is to be melted. If vise grips are available, use them as a handle when pouring; the can may slip from the grasp of pliers at a critical moment. I heat the lead on the kitchen stove. As the lead melts, use a stick to push the slag and dirt away from the pour spout. Continue to heat the lead for another two or three minutes after it has all melted because when you pour, it cools fast! Position the mold over a protective surface and when all is ready, pour. Start at one end and keep moving along as you fill the mold to the edges. In a minute or two the mold can be cooled in water and the preformed lead weight will usually fall free.

You now have mass balance weight in the form of the leading edge of your airfoil. Clean up any irregularities on the flat surface (the back side of the weight) with a file or coarse grit sandpaper. Weigh the cast part and measure its length. For talking purposes, let's say your piece is two inches long and weighs one ounce, which means that it weighs one-half ounce per running inch of length. Now let's further say that it has been determined that each blade requires one-half ounce of weight. From the above we know that one running inch of preformed lead is needed. Figure 9-24 shows a satisfactory way to install the weight.

Cut two lengths of the lead as nearly identical as possible and predrill for a couple of small brads as shown in the sketch. Carefully cut the leading edge out to fit the weight as accurately as possible. When all is ready, mix some two-part epoxy. Coat all mating surfaces of lead and wood, slip the lead weight into the cutout, and tap in the brads until the weight and brads are fully seated. Use any

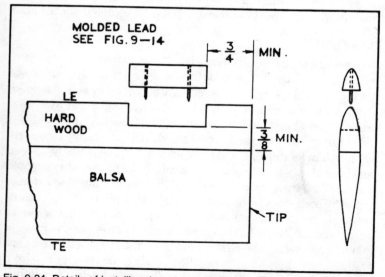

Fig. 9-24. Details of installing the pre-shaped lead mass balance weight.

Fig. 9-25. Blade tip with mass balance added. A discarded blade has been cut off through the lead weight to show the attachment details.

leftover epoxy to fill and smooth any open cracks or low places. When fully hard, sand the surfaces, starting with a block and coarse grit paper and ending with a fine grit. The finished product is a strong, efficient way to move the blade CG forward, and when completed, the weight is practically impossible to see (Fig. 9-25). I have found that after a little practice, six composite blades with weights can be mass-produced in about six and one-half to seven hours; for one-piece blades for smaller machines, six blades require about three hours excluding painting.

BALANCING ROTOR ASSEMBLIES

It is quite difficult to make blades that all have exactly the same spanwise CG position or weight. This is, therefore, one advantage of making up a number of blades at a time. You may be able to pair them up, which will make balancing of the rotor assembly easier.

An accurate balance of the entire rotor assembly, including the control rotor, is very important from the standpoint of reliable radio operation and minimal mechanical wear. It should be noted that the rotor balancing instructions in some commercial R/C kits are not entirely accurate. For example, the rotor may *not* be accurately balanced merely because the assembly, when resting on the control rotor arms if disturbed on the balance stand, returns to an approximately level position. This *does* indicate that the center of gravity of the assembly is *below* the suspension points—that is, the system is stable, somewhat like a pendulum. If the CG is *well* below the suspension, the assembly becomes quite insensitive to an out-of-balance condition. It, therefore, follows that the best possible balance can be achieved if the entire assembly including the control rotor is suspended at the vertical CG of the rotor assembly. This is usually quite difficult to do, especially if the rotor has an underslung head in which the control rotor is positioned above the assembly CG.

A far more accurate balance procedure involves a straight-through arbor (shaft), usually the same diameter as the rotor shaft, rolling on level knife edges (Fig. 9-26). The scratchbuilder will be very much better off in the long run to design his rotor head with such balance provisions. It is true that a teetering rotor with an underslung head and a control rotor is inherently more difficult to design for straight-through balance shaft provisions—*more* difficult, but by no means impossible. There are, in fact a number of teetering head kits presently on the market that, with some minor modifications, could be adapted to this type of balance. All types of the head would require some kind of machined spacers or collars to clamp the hub rigid and normal to the shaft only during the balancing procedure. The control rotor may be balanced as an integral part of the assembly by using an arbor which extends only partway through, using one of the alternate knife edge arrangements shown in Fig. 9-27. This method of balancing plus what is called "tracking" assures that the rotor is not only statically but dynamically balanced as well.

An object may be *statically* balanced, and then when rotated it is

Fig. 9-26. When the main and tail rotors are balanced this way, and the main rotor is in track, the model will not shudder when it is hovered.

136

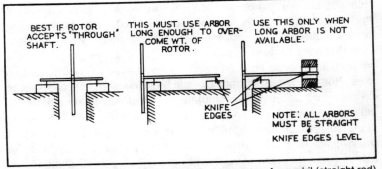

Fig. 9-27. There are several ways to balance any rotor. A mandril (straight rod) running through the rotor and sitting on *level* knife edge is by far the most accurate. The balanced rotor should stay in any position it is placed in any of the three configurations shown.

also in *dynamic* balance; or a statically balanced object may have very poor dynamic balance. A great many tire shops will try to tell you they are dynamically balancing a wheel just because they rotate it when performing the work, when they are actually performing a *static* balance. Let's look at a couple of examples and I think the above babbling will become quite clear. Consider a racing bicycle wheel with a small tire. In such an object, essentially all the parts which move at high tangential velocity lie in a common plane. If the wheel is balanced *statically*—that is, by weighting the rim here or there so that the wheel will rest at any position in which it is placed—then the wheel will be dynamically balanced as well, and will have essentially no vibration when turned rapidly.

Now consider the cylinder shown in Fig. 9-28 which has a rotational axis through the cylinder. Now then, let's do a static balance on the cylinder by placing the axis (shaft) on knife edges. Let's say that the cylinder always comes to rest with point (x) at the bottom. Furthermore, we find that by adding a certain amount of weight to position (y), the cylinder will remain in equilibrium in any position on the level knife edges. The cylinder is now *statically* balanced.

Now let's rotate the drum at high speed. It may be smooth, or it may tear itself out of the bearing supports from high vibration. Why? *Because we statically balanced it, but did not dynamically balance it.* Figure 9-17 shows what actually happened. We added the proper weight diametrically opposite, but from the static balance we had no knowledge of where the weight should be located *axially* so as not to create an upsetting moment! Similarly, unless the tire balance indicates not only where around the rim to add a given amount of weight, but also how the weight should be *distributed* between the inner and outer rim, the machine is a static balancer! What (you ask) does this have to do with rotors? Well, just this! We can balance a rotor on an arbor on knife edges. This gives *static* balance about two axes. Now the rotor is rather like the bicycle wheel in proportion of diameter to thickness. To complete the picture and have a dynamic balance, we need only to bring the rotating blades into the same plane to prevent unwanted moments (vibration). This is called *tracking the rotor*. A rigid rotor out of track (that is, in which the blades fly in different planes) will vibrate badly in all flight conditions because it is not dynamically balanced. A teetering rotor, by contrast, will tolerate an out-of-track condition a little better in hover because no moment can be transmitted from the hub into the shaft. In forward flight, however, each time the high blade (the blade that flies higher due to more lift) comes around to the advancing side, a clean vertical bump occurs.

When adding weight to one blade of a rotor assembly to balance it, the weight may be added at the tip or at the blade attachment bolt (or bolts). If added at the bolts, more lead will be required, of course, but it is far more convenient to add it here.

TAIL ROTOR BALANCE

No R/C model tail rotor has coning built-in. Most are of the single bolt attachment type, and this is good design. Since there is no coning or teetering in these tail rotors, a static balance is the same as a dynamic balance. I prefer to keep the blade retention bolts just snug enough to hold their in-plane position (I can think of

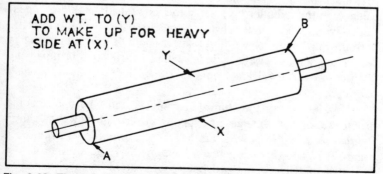

Fig. 9-28. The text describes the difference between static and dynamic balances. With a bicycle, they are the same. With the above shaft, they are quite different.

nothing sillier than to see an R/C tail rotor come to a stop and watch the "ears" droop like a tired rabbit) and yet the bolts should be free enough to permit the blades to seek their in-plane equilibrium position and also "give" under impact. I mount the new tail rotor on a shaft which is then chucked up in a drill press. The drill press is started with a slack belt (to avoid devastating acceleration) and then the belt is slowly tightened by rotating the gimbal-mounted motor. When the tail rotor is up to full operating speed, the drill press motor is turned off and the tail rotor is allowed to slowly decelerate until it stops. The assembly is then carefully removed from the drill press without disturbing the blade positions and the assembly is statically balanced on level knife edges. Usually a washer or two under the nut is all that is needed and the tail rotor is ready to install.

TRACKING THE ROTOR

From time to time I fun around with you, but what I'm about to tell you is very serious business—*very* serious indeed. *Never,* under any circumstances, point a model into the wind when holding the tail boom and increasing power (or RPM)! Many modelers track their helicopter rotors by this procedure, holding the tail boom and sighting the tips of the advancing blades (the blades going away from the holder) as they increase RPM, but they *point the model downwind*. Why not into the wind? Well, it's that old bugaboo, negative angle-of-attack stability characteristic inherent with all rotors. If the model is pointed into the wind and the lift is increased while holding the tail boom, the angle of attack will increase, which increases the lift, which increases the angle of attack still more, and suddenly the machine is up, back, and straight into the one holding the tail boom, all in a second or two! If the model is pointed downwind and held while increasing the power, the angle of attack

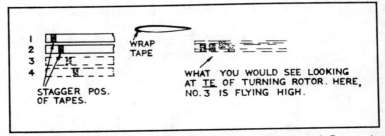

Fig. 9-29. One method of tracking a blade (any number of blades). Be sure to stagger the position of the tape, and keep your gaze at the trailing edge side of the rotor *very short!*

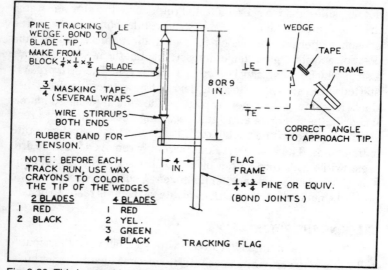

Fig. 9-30. This is a tracking method that is more work but far safer because you don't have to put your eyes in the tip-path-plane. When I first worked with full-size helicopters, this is the *only* way we had to check track. (What we didn't realize was that a rotor in track in hover would go way out of track at high speed, but that is beyond us here.)

decreases as the nose comes up—which means that it has no tendency to increase lift further.

If you feel you must track using this procedure, remember two things: Keep out of the tail rotor and minimize the time that your face is in line with the tip-path-plane (I have seen two blades come off at rated RPM)! The bottom line—have respect for all parts turning at high speeds.

Suppose one blade is flying a half inch higher than the other one (or more). How do you identify which blade it is when the rotor has stopped turning? One easy way is to cut pieces of half-inch electrical tape and position them from the leading to trailing edge of each blade as shown in Fig. 9-29. Then when you view the turning rotor from the tip-path-plane, you will see the black (or other contrasting color) strips on the side where the blades are moving away from you. Remember, keep your gaze short!

For the novice: Don't be ashamed to fasten the skids of your model securely to a table or bench (with plenty of rotor clearance) and track your R/C helicopter the old-fashioned way as shown in Fig. 9-30. The notes in the sketch are mostly self-explanatory. The big advantage with this method is that your face does not get in the plane of rotation. The procedure is to bond the wedge as shown on the tips, and then "butter" each edge with a different colored wax crayon. Be sure to approach the rotating blade tips slowly and with the tracking "flag," as it's called, in a *trailing position*, about sixty degrees or so, as shown. Slowly approach, and just as soon as you feel contact at the masking tape, immediately pull the flag away. Even with a fast reaction, you will generally have not one but two complete sets of prints. Read the clearer set, make incidence adjustments, "rebutter" the blade tips, stick on another length of tape, and you are ready for another track check. This can all be done without having to stop the engine.

WEIGHT AND BALANCE MADE EASIER

The terms *weight* and *balance* are usually used together because one effects the other. It is a definite advantage to be able to estimate, as accurately and as soon as possible, what the various parts of your new scratchbuilt helicopter will weigh and where the center of gravity of the completed machine will be located—that is, how it will balance. Although the CG is actually defined in space by three coordinates (longitudinal, lateral, and vertical), the longitudinal position is the only one that we will be concerned about. Indeed it is the only one over which we have any appreciable control. Concerning the lateral position—if the tail rotor is below the main rotor, as most are, you might want to locate the batteries on the advancing blade side. This is to offset the rolling moment created by the thrust of the tail rotor. It isn't all that bad, but if you have ever wondered why your helicopter always hovers one side low, that's probably the reason.

Vertically, you have very little recourse in the CG position except to make the rotor shaft longer or shorter. With a teetering rotor, the higher the rotor is above the CG, the greater the moment generated. Remember, the moment is equal to the thrust times the offset distance from the CG to the extension of the thrust line. By the same token, however, the height of the rotor above the CG determines the magnitude of the gravity moment that must be overcome. This is reviewed in Fig. 9-31.

The nose-down pitching moment is $T \times d$ or $M = (T) \times (d)$, and since the weight equals the lift, M must overcome the opposing moment $W \times l$. Here's the punchline. Regardless of the length of the rotor shaft, l_1, is to d_1 as l_2 is to d_2; mathematically, $\dfrac{l_1}{l_2} = \dfrac{d_1}{d_2}$. That is,

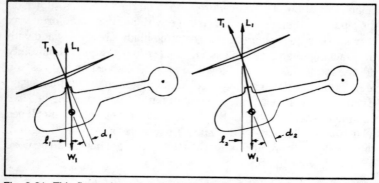

Fig. 9-31. This figure, in conjunction with the text, proves that with a flapping rotor, the length of the mast has no effect on control power.

the longer the shaft, the greater the control power, but in the same proportion, the gravity moment to be overcome is greater. Therefore, with a teetering rotor, control power is not affected by the length of the rotor shaft.

There are two ways to calculate the longitudinal CG location of a model. One involves establishing a reference datum line at the main rotor shaft, and then all items forward of the shaft have a negative moment arm (whatever that is); so if you add a positive weight at a negative moment arm, you—well, what *do* you do? The other method is to establish a reference datum line at the most forward point of the fuselage. This is always called station (STA) 0.00. This, incidentally, is the easy way. Let's assume you are designing your own helicopter. Two of several important items about which you will be concerned are to make the machine as light as possible, and to be able to predict, as accurately as possible, the longitudinal CG position. This makes it convenient to plan ahead, rearranging components as necessary, so that the final CG position is on or slightly ahead of the main rotor shaft (without having to add weight in the nose). From the sketching you have been doing and the layout, you already have a design envelope that you must cram all those goodies into. Therefore, you must know ahead of time, as accurately as possible, where that CG is going to be. Your layout of the overall side view of the machine will have station lines superimposed on the drawing which locate centers of components or subassemblies. It should look something like that of Fig. 9-32, which is my scratchbuilt rigid rotor Cheyenne.

Let's prepare a weight and balance chart with four columns having the following headings: *Item, Weight, Moment arm,* and

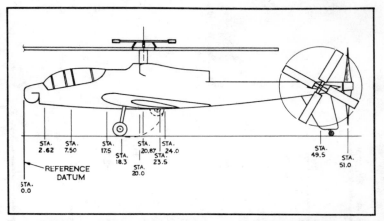

Fig. 9-32. When designing a new model, set up a weight and balance table. Make a drawing of the side view of the ship and call the tip of the nose station 0.0. Then, as you locate components, weigh them and measure the distance from STA 0.0. The text shows a typical wt. and bal. table.

Moment. Now list in column 1, under *Item*, all the components of the machine. It is obvious that the more you break each assembly down into subassemblies, and each of these into component parts and details, the more accurate your CG location estimate will be. Furthermore, it will be to your advantage as you obtain or make parts to weigh them, continually update your weight and balance chart.

For the exercise in the included weight and balance table (Table 9-2), I have primarily stayed with assemblies to simplify proceedings. For example, the power plant assy., which is dropped into place as a unit in the Cheyenne, is listed as a sample item with one weight and at one station. The scratchbuilder is advised to break this down into the individual components (Fig. 9-33), each with its own weights (as weighed or first estimate). Then from your master layout, determine the location of each item—that is, how many inches aft of the reference datum line.

Now then, for each item in column 1, you have a weight in ounces in column 2, and a moment arm in inches from the reference datum in column 3. Next, for each item, multiply the weight (2) times the arm (3) and enter the product in column 4. Now add up all the weights in column 2, and also add up all the moments in column 4. Finally, divide the sum of column 4 by the sum of column 2. The quotient, or answer, is the CG position of your helicopter in inches aft of the reference datum line. In the example table of the

Table 9-2. Weight and Balance.

(1) Item	(2) Weight (ounces)	×	(3) Moment Arm from Ref. Datum Arm (inches)	=	(4) Moment (in-oz)
Powerplant incl: engine, engine mounts, fan, belt, pulleys, gears, bearings, clutch, shaft, etc.	41.5		17.5		726.25
Main rotor assy incl: rotor head, four blades, gyro assy, mast, support structure.	50.0		20.87		1043.50
Fuselage incl: airframe shell, wings, support structure, landing gear (retracted), radio, all servos.	71.0		20.0		1420.00
Tail rotor assy incl: hub, four blades, gear box, shafts, stabilizer, fin, tail wheel, etc.	8.0		49.1		392.80
Propeller assy incl: hub, three blades, pitch-change-mech., shaft.	3.0		51.0		153.0
Fuel tank, fuel, batteries	11.0		7.5		82.5
Sums	184.5 oz				3818.05 in-oz

Center of gravity (CG) $= \dfrac{(4)}{(2)} = \dfrac{3818.05}{184.5} = 20.7$ inches aft of reference datum.

Fig. 9-33. The author's Cheyenne power package including the engine, muffler, heat sink, speed-reduction pulleys, clutch, tail rotor bevel gear takeoff, and main rotor pinion gear. The whole thing was dropped into place as a unit.

Cheyenne, the CG is 20.7 inches aft of STA 0.00, whereas, the rotor assembly is at STA 20.87. The CG, therefore, is essentially where it should be—at or slightly forward of the rotor shaft.

ENGINE COOLING

There are, in general, three engine cooling configurations, each with variations on the theme. Fig. 9-34 shows a variation of

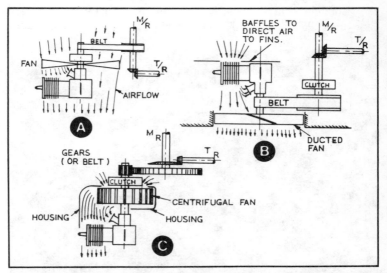

Fig. 9-34. The three most popular methods of cooling an engine. There are of course many variations on each theme.

each type. Configurations A and C sometimes have the engine mounted upright with the clutch shaft driving level gears. Configuration A is by far the simplest and lightest, involving only a small fan to pass cooling air between the cyclinder fins. It is, however, the least efficient because only the standing sector of the fan disc directly above the fins is useful in cooling the engine. The remainder of the blown air is not directed at anything in particular. Futhermore, because the engine carburetor air horn is facing the airflow, a considerable amount of "road grit" will enter the engine unless a filter is used. Dirt ingestion is inherent in all helicopters because of the high rotor downwash that impinges on the ground and then recirculates back down through the rotor again.

Configuration B positions the engine facing downward, with the fan (ducted) pulling the air past the fins which are closely baffled to force *all* the fan air through the fin area (Fig. 9-35). To be effective, the fan *must* be ducted, that is, have close wall tolerance at the tips of the blades. This system is certainly the most efficient, but is also the most complex to build and maintain because of the baffles and also the close tolerance fan duct or shroud. One other advantage is that the air horn is facing away from the incoming airflow. This serves as a dirt trap; the dirt and grit, being heavier than air, tend to continue on through the fan with only the air making the turn into the carburetor.

Configuration C is fairly efficient, as it uses a centrifugal blower to take air in axially and then sling it out against a collector

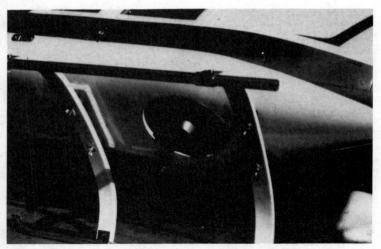

Fig. 9-35. Ducted fan is one of the best ways to cool the engine. See Fig. 9-34B.

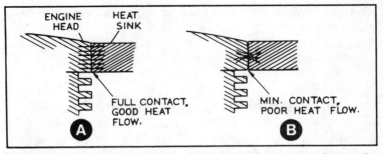

Fig. 9-36. It is important to have a good metal-to-metal contact and fit the entire depth of the heat sink for maximum cooling.

wall until it comes to the opening which deflects all the air down around the fins. In this configuration, the fins should also have baffles around them, except that they should not be as close-fitting as those with the ducted fan (configuration B), because the centrifugal air pump (commonly called the "squirrel-cage blower") will not develop as high as pressure differential as a ducted fan. If too tightly baffled, the squirrel-cage blower will tend to choke up, and will simply not move as much air. This arrangement also needs a filter for the same reason as configuration A.

All R/C helicopter engines should have heat sinks to improve the cooling efficiency of all configurations, especially with engines of .40 displacement and larger. The term *heat sink* is a bit of a misnomer. In the purest sense, a heat sink would be like a reservoir, or a bucket. That is, it would take longer to "fill up" (or heat up), but once stabilized, the temperature would be just about as high as ever. A better term to describe the extra fin cooling surface that we clamp to the engine head would be *increased cooling capability*. Heat sinks (oh well!) are readily available for most engines at hobby stores. They are also quite easy to make from ¼ or 5/16 2024 T3 aluminum plate, particularly if a special shape is needed due to space requirements.

A note of caution on heat sinks: The engine head surface must make full contact with the heat sink as illustrated in Fig. 9-36. The engine in A would run cooler than the one in B. I have, on occasion, had to remove a head that, for whatever reason, did not present a true cylindrical surface to fit the heat sink. An arbor to hold the head through the glow plug hole is adapted from a burned-out glow plug (this is only for heads with concentric plug locations).

The glow plug is screwed into the head from either side, whichever is more suitable for clamping in the lathe chuck. The glow plug hexagon flats are then mounted to run true in the lathe chuck (either three or four jaw chuck is okay for this light cut). Usually one or two passes of one or two thousands of an inch each is all that is required to achieve an acceptable heat sink fit.

TRAINING GEAR

There are a number of training gear arrangements available, all reasonably good (Fig. 9-37). Most of them increase the span of the landing gear to protect the main rotor blades from turnover damage during the hover training period. Figure 9-38 shows one more design. It is simple, lightweight, cheap, and quickly made. It requires a piece of 1×2 (actually ⅝×1⅝) inch white fir or white pine four feet long for large models and three feet long for smaller machines. A band saw and an electric hand drill with a ½ inch bit are the only tools needed.

The 1×2 is "ripped" on the band saw to make two pieces that will actually end up being about 9/32×1⅝ (by the three or four feet). Figure 9-24 is the top view of a typical skid landing gear with the training gear in place. Each piece has the shape laid out on it as shown in Fig. 9-39. Notice the crossover points at the center are different; otherwise the outlines are the same. Notice that the ½ inch holes, through which the skids slide, are angled 45 degrees. The hole is drilled straight through, then the drill is slowly angled to

Fig. 9-37. The "X" training gear was incompatible with the Cheyenne narrow wheel tread. This "hula hoop" served nicely. Incidently, after the hoop was removed the Cheyenne showed absolutely no lateral turnover tendency because the rigid rotor and gyro stabilized it.

148

Fig. 9-38. The "X" training skids with which the author learned to fly his Jet-Ranger.

the 45 degree slant (while turning, of course). The drill is angled one way for both holes in one skid and the other way for both holes in the other skid. When sawed and drilled as shown in Fig. 9-40, one set will weigh about four to six ounces. No finish is necessary.

To install, feed the top skid (the one with the bridge in the center) over the forward end of the left-hand landing gear tube. Slide it back and engage the aft end of the right-hand landing gear tube in the aft hole of the training skid. Then slide the training skid all the way forward. Now repeat the above procedure to install the other skid. The bridge of the first skid should just clear the second one when it is installed and both training skids are moved forward.

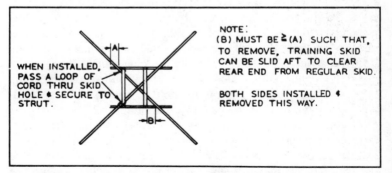

Fig. 9-39. One method of making a light, strong, and cheap training gear. The entire gear can be made using a band saw and a length of one by two inch white fir or white pine.

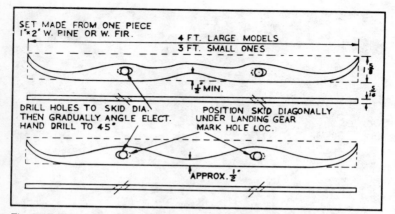

Fig. 9-40. This shows the general shape. Note carefully the holes and how they are slanted. See Fig. 9-39.

The model should sit level on the pavement without any appreciable rocking.

One final step: Pass a short length of cord through the hole and around the rear strut and tie it. Do this on both sides to prevent the training skids from sliding aft and falling off in flight. The attractive feature of this training gear is that it is low cost and quickly made. This training gear is *not* for use in grass, but when used on hard pavement, it will save many rotor blades during the early hover training days.

DRILLING HOLES

Nothing is more discouraging than completing a work piece in which the drilled holes do not line up with those of mating parts. A good solution is to drill on assembly wherever possible. When this is not possible, refer to your design layout, and using drafting dividers and/or a steel hundredths scale, "lift" the hole location from the layout and transfer it into the work material. A light tap on a carefully located center punch completes the hole positioning. If the exact location, size, and shape of a hole is important, *never* hand-hold either the drill or the part to be drilled.

Another suggestion before drilling: After you have "dimpled" the hole location with a center punch, the dimple looks something like the magnified cross-section in Fig. 9-41. The punch displaces the material out of the dimple to form a tiny crater around the center. It is difficult to start a drill in the hole location at the left. Very often the drill will "walk" around the outside of the crater. To prevent this, and also to visually define the center more clearly, run a file or fine sanding block over the surface to remove the crater rim as shown at the right of the figure.

Before drilling the hole, the work should be mounted in a drill press vise or clamped onto a flat wood base. In either case, the work and its mounting base must be securely clamped to the drill press table. I use a small drill (about number 55 to 60), in the chuck to center on the hole location. When it *is* centered, the table locked, and all clamps secure, the tiny drill is removed and a centering drill is clamped in the chuck. The first revolution is hand-turned, holding light pressure to check whether the centering drill does, in fact, coincide with the hole's intended center. The hole is started; the centering is then replaced by the required final drill bit, and the hole is finally drilled. Used crankcase oil is a good drill coolant.

Location of the hole and setup time to drill only one hole may take 10-15 minutes or so, whereas the actual drilling may take 20-30 seconds! The hole is however more likely to be located where it is intended.

TAPPING HOLES

When tapping a hole in aluminum, if you have any choice, select the National Coarse (NC) threads rather than National Fine (NF), especially in the smaller sizes (2-56, 3-48, 4-40, etc.). The course thread holds much better in aluminum. Also, you will notice in the published drill sizes for tapped holes, the recommended drill size to tap a given hole provides 75 percent of the full thread. It is advisable to use the recommended size drill for thread sizes #2, #3, and probably #4. For threads larger than #4, however, you can usually

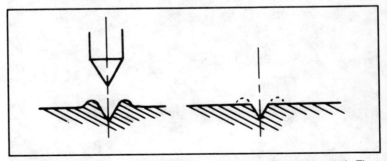

Fig. 9-41. When drilling a hole, locate the exact center with a center punch. Then using a file or sandpaper dress down the displaced metal around the dimple. It is easier to see the center, and the drill (if you don't have a center drill) will stay in the dimple.

151

use one or two drill sizes smaller than that recommended. For example, a 6-32 thread calls out a #36 (.1065) drill. This would be correct for a steel bolt in a steel part, but in aluminum, a steel bolt will hold better if a #38 (.1015) drill is used. This provides better gripping power without the danger of "bottoming" the tap in the hole because the standard root diameter of the 6-32 thread is .0974 inch which is smaller than the #38 (.1015) drill. Crankcase drainings are an excellent tap lubricant also.

MILLING

If you are able to obtain some end mills (surplus stores) or even a selection of rotary files, you can do a surprisingly good job of milling, using your drill press. Figures 9-42 and 9-43 show a couple of setups. *Caution:* Always hand-feed the work *against* rotation of the cutter. Figure 9-44 shows what happened when my mind wandered and I hand-fed the work into the cutter *with* rotation!

STRESS CONCENTRATION

When a part is carrying a high load (bending or tension), and it has abrupt changes in shape and/or size (sharp corners, holes, cutouts, etc.), very high stress loads will concentrate around the corners, etc., and catastrophic failure *can* result. One of several good "rules of thumb" is: Avoid sharp corners; in particular, avoid *concave* sharp corners on all parts you suspect may carry high loads.

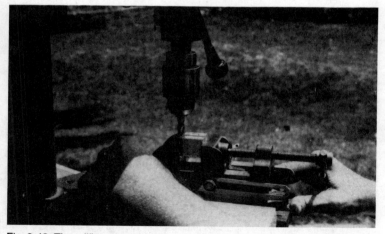

Fig. 9-42. The milling operation. Remember to feed *against* rotation. Go slowly and take light cuts and you can do a very satisfactory job. The vise must have guide blocks clamped on both sides.

Fig. 9-43. Curved surfaces can be milled by mounting the work on a pivoting platform. The platform is hand rotated about the bolt, which is the center of the arc.

One part to watch for in some models is the feathering spindle that extends out of the hub and retains the blade. Such a spindle is shown in Fig. 9-45. The concave sharp corner at the inboard side of the set-screw groove carries a very high stress (at the point of the arrow). I've had one fail in flight! New spindles were made, in which the sharp groove was replaced by a cylindrical depression with no sharp corners. These smooth set-screw "dimples," or depressions, are easily made by mounting the spindle in a drill press vise and, using a small rotary file, milling these indentations as shown. It takes just a few minutes, and no more problems in that area!

Fig. 9-44. This is what happened when my mind wandered and I fed the work into the cutter *with* rotation.

153

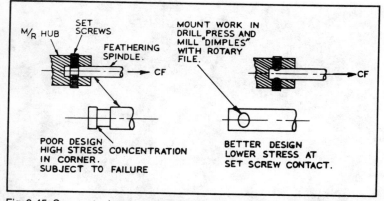

Fig. 9-45. Some rotor heads on model kits use feathering spindles held in place as shown at left. Very high stress concentration occurs at the inner corner as shown. I had one fail in the corner with the model hovering at 20 ft., and I found the blade 100 feet away. A much better design is shown at the right. No failures and no spindles have ever pulled out.

MOUNTING BEARINGS

Designing and machining ball bearing supports, as commonly used all over helicopters, is easier than you may think. Most all R/C model bearing mounts are aluminum, and are made from either 3/16 or ¼ inch plate. The diameter is turned in a lathe so that the ball bearing outer race will just begin to start into the prepared hole when pushed by hand. The bearing can be held in place several ways, so even if you goof and make the mounting hole too big so that the bearing "falls" in, don't despair. A little *blue* (don't use red) thread-friction-lock fluid placed carefully on the outside of the outer race and in the mating recess will usually hold it in place.

Another way is to insert the bearing and then, using a center punch, stake it as shown in Fig. 9-46. This works particularly well if the edge of the bearing is recessed slightly below the aluminum support so that the center punch causes a cold-flow distortion of the support to trap the bearing.

Another way that works well, particularly if the axial load is light, is to use a close-fitting brass tubing spacer on the shaft that is the correct length to prevent binding or drift. I try to stay away from supports that are shrink fits on the bearings. Without expensive and precise measuring equipment, it is difficult to obtain the proper shrink fit without danger of damaging the bearing by binding.

One other point on mounting bearings: You may wish to use a bearing in another model at a later time. You should provide a means

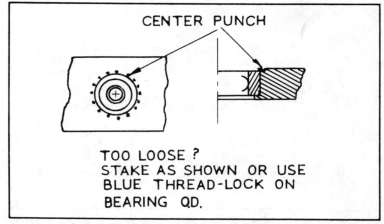

CENTER PUNCH

TOO LOOSE ?
STAKE AS SHOWN OR USE
BLUE THREAD-LOCK ON
BEARING QD.

Fig. 9-46. A couple of suggestions on how to mount ball bearings.

to remove the bearing from its old support. Figure 9-47 shows the wrong and right ways to design a bearing shoulder.

NONMETALLIC GEARS

A nonmetallic gear (for example, the main rotor shaft bull gear) can be a problem to mount in such a way as to avoid excessive stress concentration. Figure 9-48 shows the wrong and the right ways to accomplish this.

There are several good supply houses that carry a complete line of miniature hardware for radio-controlled helicopter power-trains. I have purchased gears, bearings, belts, pulleys, etc., from Stock Drive Products, 55 Denton Street, New Hyde Park, NY 11040.

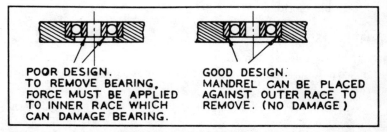

POOR DESIGN.
TO REMOVE BEARING,
FORCE MUST BE APPLIED
TO INNER RACE WHICH
CAN DAMAGE BEARING.

GOOD DESIGN.
MANDREL CAN BE PLACED
AGAINST OUTER RACE TO
REMOVE. (NO DAMAGE)

Fig. 9-47. In some kits, the ball bearing assembly is mounted such that high force must be applied to the inner race to force it out. This can ruin the bearing by distorting the race or ball surface just enough to make it unusable. The setup at the right is better. A mandril, piece of steel tubing, or even a socket wrench can be used to press the outer race out without any damage.

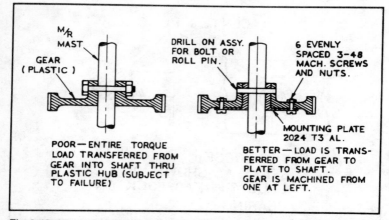

Fig. 9-48. A poor way (left) a one good way (right) to mount a nonmetallic gear to the main rotor shaft. High torque is transmitted from the gear to the shaft and there must be a strong path to carry this torque.

GEAR SETUPS

When mating two gears, be sure that they have the *same* tooth pitch angle. It is okay to mate a metallic pinion (small) gear to a non-metallic large diameter gear, but the reverse is not good. If the pinion gear is nonmetallic, each tooth will make many more contacts (because it is smaller), and because it is softer material, it will fail quite early.

When setting up two gears, check to see that they run freely (do not bottom). Also, check to see that they are not too far apart. If so, full tooth contact will not occur, which in turn causes high bending stress and possibly early failure. When two gears are properly set up, with one held solid, the other should have a barely perceptible motion.

MATERIALS

The question often arises as to what kinds of materials to use for what functions. I have found the following to be generally acceptable:

- ☐ Steel or brass pinion on "Nylon," "Delrin," or equivalent gears.
- ☐ Brass on brass for small bevel gears (tail rotor gears, etc.).
- ☐ Aircraft steel (4130) for tail rotor drive shafts, clutch shafts, main rotor spindles, etc. (usually made from aircraft bolts).

☐ Drill rod (150,000 to 180,000 PSI) ultimate tensile strength (F_{t_u})-main rotor shaft.

☐ Aluminum 2024 T3 sheet, plate, bar etc., for general purpose. It is plentiful, easy to work, and has high strength. Stay away from 7075 T6 aluminum. It is exceptionally strong but is subject to cracking from even a small scratch. This characteristic is known as "high notch sensitivity."

If your scratchbuilt helicopter has an aluminum tube tail boom, and you are wondering how you are going to support the tail rotor drive shaft at mid-span, consider the following. It works well. Cut off a length of hardwood dowel, broom stick, etc., and sand or turn in the lathe until it just slides into the tail boom. Use the lathe *chuck* to hold the dowel. Before removing it from the chuck, drill a concentric hole (use a drill that is one drill *number* larger than the intended shaft). The hole should be about two inches deep. Now cut off two sections of the wood dowel, each about ¾ inch long, and with a centering drill, "bell" one end as shown in Fig. 9-49. A music wire .0935 inch diameter, is fine for the shaft (Fig. 9-50). The hole should be #41 (.096). You will have no trouble at all in blindly feeding the shaft through two supports such as these (be sure the "bell" ends face the same direction).

For your next scratchbuilt that uses feathering bearings, consider adding a thrust bearing to carry the very high centrifugal load. If heavy tip weights are used, the thrust bearings reduce the feathering friction which may occur as the result of binding in the radial bearings if they are overloaded in the axial direction. Installation is quite simple, as seen in Fig. 9-51 through 9-53. The thrust bearings

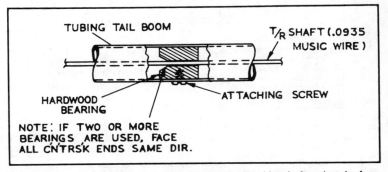

Fig. 9-49. For the smaller helicopters using a tail rotor driveshaft and a tube for a boom, this hard wood dowel turned down and drilled works well to keep the shaft from whipping. Countersink and install with the countersink toward the end from which you feed in the shaft. You will have no trouble at all in installing it.

Fig. 9-50. If your JetRanger needs a new tail rotor driveshaft, this is an easy and accurate way to make the ends flat. The author uses .0935 music wire (hobby shop) with the ends milled to .057 inch thick (check with micrometer) and about ¾ inch long.

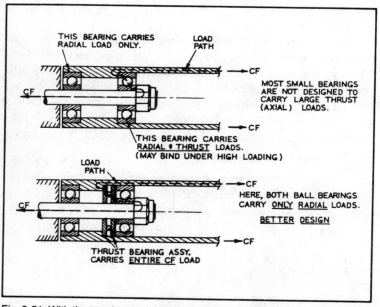

Fig. 9-51. With the trend toward rigid rotors some builders are using blades with high tip mass balance. This imposes very high *axial* loads on *radial* bearings not designed to take high loads. To avoid binding or failure, try inserting an additional thrust bearing to take *all* the axial load. See Fig. 9-53.

Fig. 9-52. A typical simple scratchbuilt tail rotor gearbox. Brass tubing on the rotor shaft accurately positions the miter gear.

are obtainable from the same suppliers as the gears, etc. Incidentally, where possible, use *sealed* radial bearings to keep out road grit, etc.

Landing gear struts and skids can be made quite easily from ½ inch diameter × .031 wall 2024 T3 aluminum tubing. They are lightweight and very strong. An inexpensive tube bender, consist-

Fig. 9-53. The thrust bearing (center right just outboard of the pitch link) takes *all* of the blade centrifugal force so there is no danger of the radial bearing binding (See Fig. 9-51). The center punch dot on the bearing block is to serialize the part for identification.

ing of a tightly wound coil spring that has a slide fit over the tube, can be purchased (along with the tubing) at most good surplus metal supply houses (Fig. 9-54).

Before bending, it is a good idea to draw out, full-size, on paper the final desired shape. Next, place the spring on the tube and center it over the area where you wish the tightest part of the bend to be, and apply the bending force to the tube by hand. It is a good idea to provide a few extra inches of tubing at the end for a better hand hold. The excess is cut off the finished strut or skid later.

The typical one-piece curved strut shown in Fig. 9-55 will be much stronger if it is attached to the airframe by straps, rather than by bolts through the strut.

The "friction nuts" that are furnished with some kits are excellent. If, after repeated removal, you find they have lost their friction, apply a drop of *blue* thread-friction-liquid. Apply this liquid to all nuts or bolts on all parts of the helicopter every time a nut or bolt is removed and reinstalled. Never use the red liquid, incidentally, unless you absolutely *know* that you will never have any reason to remove it (because you probably won't be able to)!

First, never scribe (scratch) a line that you do not intend to cut. Use a pencil here. If you are laying out a shape to be sawed or milled, try this: Scribe the lines and then take a childs' wax crayon (blue or black) and color the areas where the scribed lines are. Then scrub *across* each line. You will clean the surface but leave the scribed lines darkly marked.

PREFLIGHT PROCEDURE

Before each flying session, clean all accessible gears. A common cotton swab or a toothbrush dipped in isopropyl alcohol works well. This effort is particularly important with non-metallic gears,

Fig. 9-54. An easy way to bend tube (without crimping) for landing gear struts or skids.

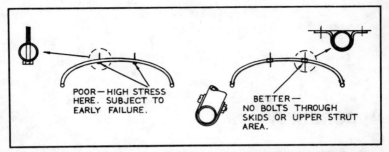

Fig. 9-55. A poor way (left) and a better way (right) to install tubular landing gear struts. It takes a few minutes more, but the struts will last much longer.

which are likely to have road grit becoming imbedded in the surface of the teeth causing excessive wear and premature failure.

Also, before a flight, wipe down all blades with a clean rag. The difference between clean, smooth blades, or dirty, rough blades can add up, in wasted horsepower, to the weight of the fuel the model is carrying.

POSTFLIGHT INSPECTION

After each flying session, wipe off all excess external oil and fuel, and pump the tank dry. Look the model over for anything amiss. You will be surprised at what you will find sometimes, for example: loose control rod-ends, teeth missing from a belt or gear, loose main or tail rotor feather bearing spindles, loose belt tension, loose carburetor, etc.

Appendix A

Symbols and Nomenclature

a_o Rotor coning *angle* created by moments due to lift and centrifugal forces in equilibrium—*degrees.*

A   Area-*ft.*

b   Number of blades on a rotor

B   Blade tip-loss factor. A function of blade loading, and therefore, the number of blades, as well as gross weight—*no dimension.* B=.96 is a reasonable average value for R/C models.

c   Blade chord—must be converted into *feet* when used in equations. Hence a 2 inch chord $= \frac{2}{12}$ or .166 ft.

c   (also) Blade flapwise damping coefficient—*no dimension.*

c_c Blade *critical* flapwise damping coefficient; c_c will not sustain vibration past one half cycle—*no dimension.*

c_x; C_x Any dimensionless coefficient expressed as a ratio of two quantities. The subscript denotes the subject or function.

$\overline{c}_l$ Rotor *blade mean lift* coefficient in hover.

C_T = rotor thrust coefficient; $C_T = \dfrac{T}{\pi R^2 \rho (\Omega R)^2}$

C_Q Rotor torque coefficient; $C_{Q_i} + C_{Q_o} = \dfrac{Q}{\pi R^2 \rho (\Omega R)^2 R}$

C_{Q_i} Torque coefficient due to induced power to produce lift; approx. equals

$$\frac{C_T \frac{3}{2}}{1.358} \quad = \quad \frac{\sqrt{C_T^3}}{1.358}$$

C_{Q_o} Torque coefficient due to profile power to rotate blades.

CF   Centrifugal *force*. Created when a body is rotated—*pounds*. omega — RPM

$$= \frac{w}{g} \Omega^2 r_{cG} \quad \text{(for blade with tip weights)}$$
$$= \frac{w}{g} \Omega^2 \frac{R}{\sqrt{3}} \text{ (blade with no tip weights)}$$

CG   Center of gravity, usually identified as "xx" inches from some reference line.

d   Any distance dimension—*inches or feet.*

D   Rotor diameter—*feet.*

F   Force-*pounds.*

g   Acceleration of gravity, (on earth) approx. 32.2 feet per sec. per sec. $(ft/sec)^2$.

I_f Moment of Inertia of a *free* flapping blade about its hinge point; $\frac{1}{3} M R^2$—*lb sec²ft.*

k   Blade centrifugal restoring *moment*; $\frac{1}{3} M \Omega^2 R^2$—*ft lbs.*

l   Any length—*ft.*

M	Moment. This is a strange term used to describe a force times a distance. Example: If a 100-lb. diver stands on the end of an 8 foot diving board at its attachment point is subjected to 100 ₆ 8 or 800 ft-pounds *moment*.
M	(Also) Mass of an object—*slugs on earth.* $M = \dfrac{w}{g} = \dfrac{w}{32.2}$.
N_R	Reynolds Number—*no dimension.* A mathematical description of the state of the flow of a viscous fluid around a body. A function of velocity, density and viscosity of the fluid and the *length* of the body. $N_R = \dfrac{v \times 1}{.000157}$ for R/C models. $N_R = \dfrac{2\,\pi(\text{RPM})(R)(C)}{(60)(.000157)}$ for a hovering rotor tip.
P	Pressure. $\dfrac{F}{A} - \dfrac{LBS}{FT^2}$ or PSF
P_i	Rotor induced power— $\dfrac{\text{ft-lbs}}{\text{sec}}$ or HP
P_o	Rotor profile power— $\dfrac{\text{ft-lbs}}{\text{sec}}$ or HP
P_p	Parasite power (airframe, landing gear, stabilizers, fins, etc.)— $\dfrac{\text{ft-lbs}}{\text{sec}}$ or HP.
Q	Rotor torque—*lb-ft.*
r	Distance from center of rotation to a point (any) on a rotor blade—*ft.*
R	Rotor radius (center to tip)—*ft.* Also, a force Resultant.
S	Stress $= \dfrac{F}{A}$ —*psi.* (inches used when calc. stress rather than *ft*, as in pressure).

S_s Shear stress $= \dfrac{F}{A} = \dfrac{\text{Transverse force}}{\text{Cross Section Area}}$ —*psi.*

S_T Tension Stress $= \dfrac{F}{A} = \dfrac{\text{Axial Force}}{\text{Cross Section Area}}$ —*psi.*

SF   Safety factor. This factor will be applied to all calc. loads to insure a safe design. In this book, SF=3 for all work.

SAS   Stability Augmentation System.

T   Thrust force of rotor—*lbs.*

V   Velocity—*feet per sec (fps).*

V_i Induced velocity—*fps.*

V_T Rotor tip tangential velocity—*fps* $= \Omega R$

w   Weight of a rotor blade (or any other *component*)—*lbs.*

W   Helicopter weight (equals T in hover)—*lbs.*

IGE   In Ground Effect hover. Hovering less than approx. 1½ rotor diameters (IGE) above ground requires substantially less power than does OGE.

OGE   Out of Ground Effect hover. More than 1½ rotor dia above ground.

GREEK LETTERS USED

α (alpha)   Blade angle of attack—*radians* (one radian = 57.3 degrees). Also rotor angle of attack—*radians.*

σ (sigma)   Rotor solidity $= \dfrac{bcR}{\pi R^2} = \dfrac{bc}{\pi R}$—*no dimension.*

π (pi)   Ratio of circumference of a circle to its diameter. Approx. 3.14—*no dimension.*

ρ	(rho)	Air density—*slugs per ft³* =.0024 standard air at Sea level (approx.).
θ	(theta)	Phase angle around azimuth between input and response. Also blade pitch angle-radians
μ	(mu)	Advance ratio$=\dfrac{V \cos oc}{\Omega R}$—no dimension we can simplify; (for models) to $\dfrac{.965\,V}{\Omega R}$.
μ	(also)	Fluid dynamic viscosity.
Δ	(delta)	Any increment (general).
Δ_3	(delta three)	The angle in degrees that the teeter axis is skewed around to create a coupling of flapping and feathering. Δ_3 is (+) if coupling decreases feathering.
λ	(lambda)	Scale factor for dynamic similarity.
v	(nu)	Kinematic coefficient of viscosity $=\dfrac{\mu}{\rho}=.000157$ (for standard air).
ψ	(PSI)	Blade position relative to airframe when looking down on rotor. $\psi = $ o (aft); $\psi = 90$ degrees (advancing); $\psi = 180$ degrees (forward); $\psi = 270$ degrees (retreating) positions—*degrees*.
ω_N	(omega-lower case)	Natural frequency of a vibrating body.
ω	(also)	Pitch or roll rate of the helicopter airframe—*radians per sec.*
Ω	(omega)	Rotor speed—*radians per sec.* $=\dfrac{RPM \times 2\pi}{60}$.

Appendix B

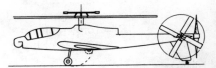

Basic Rotor Design

As stated in Chapter 9 (Design) you probably have your engine and radio, and have very probably built an R/C kit—and now you are ready to design your own helicopter. After careful thought you will decide on the type of machine it is going to be, and the general size. That is, it is going to be a bolt-together trainer, or a stand-off scale, and you will have a first estimate of the gross weight.

There are three particular design parameters, the values of which are greatly influenced by the basic mission of the model—what kind of flying that you anticipate it will do. From Chapter 9 you recall these parameters to be:

☐ Disc loading.
☐ *Blade mean lift* coefficient.
☐ Rotor solidity.

With these three parameters plus the first estimate of gross weight and the desired number of blades, you can readily calculate the rotor design as follows.

First calculate the rotor diameter;

$$\text{by } D = 2 \sqrt{\frac{W}{\pi(\text{Disc loading})}}$$

where:
D = rotor diameter-ft
W = estimated wt of helicopter

$\pi = 3.14$ (a constant)

disc loading selected from Chapter 9

Having the rotor diameter, you can now calculate the blade chord as follows:

$$C = \frac{\sigma \pi R}{b}$$

where:

C = blade chord-ft

σ = solidity selected from Chapter 9.

R = rotor radius-ft

b = number of blades desired

And now you can calculate the rotor tip speed from:

$$V_T = \sqrt{\frac{6 W}{\overline{C}_L C R b \rho}}$$

where:

V_T = tangential speed of rotor tip—ft/sec.

$\overline{C}_L$ = blade mean lift coefficient (from Chapter 9)

And finally, the rotor RPM is obtained:

$$RPM = \frac{30 V_T}{\pi R}$$

So far, you have the engine size, a first estimate of gross weight, rotor diameter, blade chord, and rotor RPM. The next step will be to calculate the total power required for the model to hover at the estimated weight. This value of power required and the calculated RPM are then compared to the engine manufacturer's power curve data to verify that the engine being considered can, in fact, produce the required power to hover. The RPM at which the engine develops the required power can also be compared to the calculated rotor speed to give you a good idea of the speed reduction (gears or belt) from the engine shaft to the main rotor shaft. Questions as to whether the rotor diameter is large enough to lift the design weight, or whether the engine will be adequate, loom ever larger as you near completion of the design stage. It is better to answer the questions at this point, while changes can still be made, than to find out the hard way after it is built.

The following is a quick, relatively easy, and reasonably accurate way to answer the above questions. The method assumes a constant chord length, and an ideally twisted blade rotor (any number of blades). A correction will then be applied to account for the untwisted blades of our R/C rotors.

The needed equations are:

$$C_T = \frac{T}{\pi R^2 \rho (\Omega R)^2}$$

where:

C_T = overall rotor thrust coefficient
T = rotor thrust = weight-LBS
π = 3.14 constant
R = rotor radius-FT
ρ = .0024 (SL standard air)
Ω = rotor speed-radians/sec
$$= \frac{\text{RPM} \times 2\pi}{60}$$
ΩR = rotor tip speed-ft/sec

$$C_Q = \frac{Q}{\pi R^2 \rho (\Omega R)^2 R}$$

C_Q = torque coefficient
Q = rotor torque-lb ft

$$\sigma = \frac{b\,c}{\pi R}$$

σ = rotor solidity
b = number of blades
c = blade chord-ft
C_{Q_i} = torque coefficient due to induced drag

$$C_{Q_i} = \frac{C_T^{\frac{3}{2}}}{B\sqrt{2}} = \frac{\sqrt{C_T^3}}{1.358}$$

B = tip loss factor. Will vary somewhat, assumed to be .96 for R/C models.

The procedure is as follows:

1. Calculate C_T using the first estimated gross weight as equal to the thrust for hover, rotor diameter, and rotor RPM found above.

2. Divide the thrust coefficient C_T by the rotor solidity σ and the square of the tip loss factor. You therefore have:

$$\frac{C_T}{(.96)^2 \sigma} = \frac{C_T}{.922\,\sigma}$$

3. From Fig. B-1 determine the value of $\dfrac{C_{Q_0}}{\sigma}$ for the just calculated value of $\dfrac{C_T}{.922\,\sigma}$.

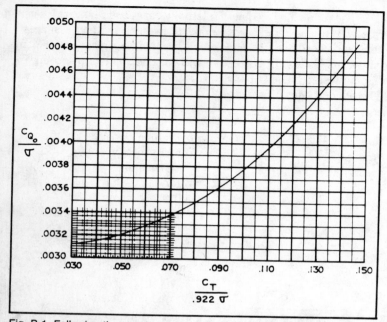

Fig. B-1. Following the step-by-step procedure, use this curve (step 3) in estimating the power required to hover. In the area most used by our present models, finer lines are shown to represent .002. The short lines are .001. Thus across the bottom using the fine lines one would read .050, .052, .054, .055, .056, .058, and .060. Using the short dashes, one would read .050, .051, .052, .053, .054, .055, etc.

4. Calculate C_{Q_o} from $\dfrac{C_{Q_o}}{\sigma^o}$ by multiplying $\dfrac{C_{Q_o}}{\sigma^o} \times \sigma = C_{Q_o}$

5. Calculate C_{Q_i} from $C_{Q_i} = \dfrac{\sqrt{C_T{}^3}}{1.358}$

6. Determine C_Q from $C_Q = C_{Q_i} + C_{Q_o}$.

7. Calculate rotor torque from:

$$Q_{TW} = C_Q\, \pi\, R^2 \rho (\Omega R)^2 R$$

Note: This is for OGE hover
TW denotes twisted blades.

8. Apply correction factor (*untwisted* blades) so that rotor torque $Q = 1.04\, Q_{TW}$.

9. Calculate total main rotor *horsepower* to hover OGE.

$$HP = \frac{2\pi(RPM)(Q)}{33000} \quad \text{*Rotor RPM}$$

170

10. A close rule of thumb says that tail rotor horsepower equals 10 percent (approx.) of the main rotor HP or $HP_{TP} = .10\ HP_{MR}$.

11. Finally we are "nickeled and dimed" by a long list of items, including cooling fans, belts, gears, and bearings, which also absorb power. The following factors are to be added to the *total rotor HP* as applicable:

drive train ball bearings	½ to 1% each
spur gear set	4% (including bearings)
level gear set (M/R)	5% each (including bearings)
belt drive	7% each
cooling fan	6-9% each
control rotor/gyro	8-10%
bevel gear set (T/R)	½% each

12. Total horsepower to hover = item 10 plus item 11.

Example: What is the power required to hover a new design helicopter having the following design characteristics:

☐ Acrobatic, bolt together.
☐ Number of main rotor blades: four.
☐ Type of rotor: rigid.
☐ No belts in drive system.
☐ First estimate of gross wt: 8.75 lbs.
☐ Engine displacement: .61 in.

From the table in Chapter 9, the above helicopter, because of its design mission, should have the following "ballpark" design parameters:

☐ Disc loading DL: .7.
☐ *Mean blade lift* coefficient $\overline{C}_L$: .25.
☐ Rotor Solidity σ: .10.

The rotor diameter should, therefore be:

$$D = 2\sqrt{\frac{W}{\pi(DL)}} = 2\sqrt{\frac{8.75}{\pi(.7)}} = 3.99 \text{ feet (assume 4 feet)}$$
$$R = 2\ ft$$

The blade chord is:

$$C = \frac{\sigma\,\pi\,R}{b} = \frac{(.10)(\pi)(2.0)}{4} = .157\ ft \text{ (or 1⅞ inches)}$$

Rotor tip speed is:

$$V_T = \sqrt{\frac{6 W}{C_L c\, R\, b\, \rho}} = \sqrt{\frac{(6)(8.75)}{(.25)(.157)(2.0)(4)(.0024)}}$$

$$= \textit{264 feet} \text{ per sec}$$

Finally, the rotor RPM is:

$$RPM = \frac{30\, V_T}{\pi\, R} = \frac{(30)(264)}{(\pi)(2)} = \textit{1260} \text{ RPM (rotor speed)}$$

Now determine the power to hover this model using the previously outlined 12 steps:

1.
$$C_T = \frac{T}{\pi R^2\, \rho\, (\Omega R)^2} \qquad \frac{8.75}{(3.14)(4)(.0024)(69696)}$$

$$C_T = .004165$$

where:

$T = W = 8.75$
$\pi = 3.14$
$R = 2$
$\rho = .0024$
$\Omega = \dfrac{1260 \times 2\pi}{60}$
$\quad = 132$ rad/sec
$(\Omega R) = 2 \times 132 = 264$
$(\Omega R)^2 = (264) \quad = 69696$

2.
$$\frac{C_T}{.922\, \sigma} = \frac{.004165}{(.922)(.10)} = .0452$$

3. From Fig. B-1, for $\dfrac{C_T}{.922\sigma}$ of .0452, $\dfrac{C_{Q_o}}{\sigma} = .00318$.

4. $C_{Q_o} = \dfrac{C_{Q_o}}{\sigma} \times \sigma = (.00318)(.1) = .000318$

5. $C_{Q_i} = \dfrac{C_T^{\frac{3}{2}}}{1.358} = \dfrac{\sqrt{(.004165)^3}}{1.358} = .000198$

6. $C_Q = C_{Q_i} + C_{Q_o} = .000198 + .000318 = .000516$

7. $Q_{TW} = C_Q\, \pi\, R^2\, \rho\, (\Omega R)^2\, R$
$= (.000516)(3.14)(4)(.0024)(69696)(2) = \textit{2.17}$ lb. ft.

8. $Q = 1.04\, Q_{TW} = (1.04)(2.17) = \textit{2.26}$ lb. ft.

9. Main Rotor Horsepower =

$$HP = \frac{2\pi \, (RPM)(Q)}{33000} = .54 \; HP$$

10. $HP_{TR} = .1 \times HP_{MR} = (.1)(.54) = .05$, so total rotor HP = .54 + .05 = $.59 \; HP$

11. Misc. friction factors times .59 added to .59:

drive train bearings $.01 \times .59 =$	.006
spur gear set (with bearings) $.04 \times .59 =$	.024
N.A.	
N.A.	
cooling fan $.06 \times .59 =$	.035
gyro (or control rotor) $.9 \times .59 =$	.053
level gear sets (T/R) $2 \times .005 \times .59 =$	.006
Total misc. friction HP =	.124

12. Total estimated horsepower to hover = .59 + .12 = $.71 \; HP$

A coment is in order at this point. Note in step 6 that C_{Q_o} is considerably greater than C_{Q_i}. This indicates that the torque due to profile power is greater than the torque due to induced power. That is, this particular rotor is not efficient in hover.

By way of contrast, the *high efficiency* design suggested in Chapter 9 for lifting heavy loads in hover, when evaluated, shows that the majority of the main rotor torque is absorbed in *induced* power, rather than profile power. This rotor would be almost 8 feet in diameter and would rotate at only about 392 RPM while lifting 15 pounds total weight (thrust) and requiring only .55 HP. Incidentally, the indications are that such a model would be subject to retreating blade stall at a comparatively low speed—on the order of 12 MPH or so.

Appendix C

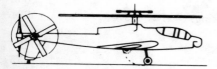

Stress Analysis

Sounds scary, doesn't it? Well, it's really not that big a deal for the R/C helicopter modeler. However, there are some areas that inherently carry high loads, and you should give these parts a bit of thought when you design them. The reason we modelers do not have to go into great detail in design strength is that our models are much stronger for their size than their larger counterparts. Drop your .40 size model (rotor not turning) from one foot height and not much will happen. Now then, if you were to drop a full-size Bell or Hiller helicopter from 10 feet (comparable scale distance), we all know that the full size machine would be severely damaged.

Metal, in general, fails in two ways: the *static* failure, such as landing gear collapsing after a hard landing, and *fatigue* failure from alternating loads such as in-plane and flapwise bending of the blade feathering spindle in forward flight. The science of predicting the magnitude of the alternating loads (which occur many times each minute) and the resulting fatigue life of a part is very complex, and is obviously beyond the intent of this book. For example, it is not at all as straightforward as the calculation of centrifugal force of a blade (which is reasonably accurate and easy).

When designing an R/C helicopter, I follow two expedient rules. First, for all parts regularly subjected to high static loads such as centrifugal force on rotor parts, a *stress concentration factor* of 3 is applied in the stress calculations. Second, for areas in which it is known that, in addition to predictable static loads, high but unknown magnitude alternating loads are also present, as with the blade feathering spindles, the next larger shank diameter, than calculated, is used (to be safe). The above is the modeler's only recourse. Let's see how it works:

Material	Type of Load Applied	Maximum Working Stress PSI
Aluminum 2024 T3	Yield stress in tension (F_{TY})	42,000 PSI
Aluminum 2024 T3	Yield stress in shear (F_{SY})	40,000 PSI
Aluminum 2024 T3	Yield stress in bearing (F_{BRY})	64,000 PSI
Steel AISI 4130	Yield stress in tension (F_{TY})	75,000 PSI
Steel AISI 4130	Yield stress in shear (F_{SY})	55,000 PSI
#6 Machine screw $F_{TU} = 125,000$ PSI	Single shear *load*	1122 LBS
#8 Machine screw $F_{TU} = 125,000$ PSI	Single shear *load*	1584 LBS
Aircraft bolt (x on head) $F_{TU} = 100,000$ PSI	Yield stress in shank (F_{TY})	82,000 PSI
Aircraft bolt (x on head) $F_{TU} = 100,000$ PSI	Yield stress in threads (F_{TY})	50,000 PSI
White pine (dry)	Tensile strength with grain	3850 PSI
White fir (dry)	Tensile strength with grain	3400 PSI
White pine (dry)	Crushing strength in bearing with grain	2800 PSI
White fir (dry	Crushing strength in bearing with grain	2700 PSI
White pine (dry)	Shear strength with grain	740 PSI
White fir (dry)	Shear strength with grain	650 PSI
White oak (dry)	Tensile strength with grain	8000 PSI
Birch plywood ("5-ply)	Tensile strength with grain bearing (tearout)	8000-10,000 PSI

Note: F_{TY} and F_{SY} are standard symbols for tensile and shear strengths, respectively.

F_{BRY} is bearing yield stress.

Material	Weight-lbs/in³
Aluminum 2024	.10
Steel 4130	.282
White pine (dry)	.016
White fir (dry)	.014
White oak (dry)	.028

Figure C-1 is a movable hub, or blade fork, of a model we are designing in Appendix B. From the design information we will

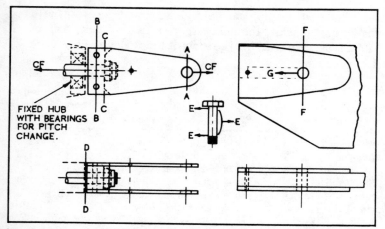

Fig. C-1. A typical bolt-together movable hub or blade fork that is easy to make using only a band saw and a drill press. We will examine any area suspected of having high stress areas subject to failure. The stress will be calculated very simply in the following pages. Figures for sections D-D and E-E are not redrawn because they are easily shown in Figure C-1.

calculate the centrifugal force on the hub due to the whirling blade. Because this force is essentially constant, it is treated as a static load.

$$CF = \frac{W}{g} \; \Omega_2 \; \frac{R}{1.73}$$

where:
CF = centrifugal force-lbs
w = weight of blade = 4.7 oz

$$CF = \frac{.294}{32.2} \; (17424) \; \frac{2}{1.73}$$

or $\frac{4.7}{16}$ = .294 lbs

CF = 184 pounds

g = gravity = 32.2 ft/sec
RPM = rotor speed = 1260 RPM
$$\Omega = \frac{2\pi(1260)}{60} = 132 \text{ rad/sec}$$
$$\Omega_2 = (132^2) = 17424$$
R = 2 ft.

Now let's look at Section A-A of Fig. C-1 (Fig. C-2). Total area of upper and lower plates at Section A-A is:

$$A = (.31-.125) \; (.04) \; (4) = .0296 \text{ in}^2$$

$$\text{Stress} = \frac{P}{A} = \frac{184}{.0296} = 6216 \text{ PSI}$$

apply SCF of 3 S = (3) (6216) = 18648

From the preceding table F_{TY} for 2024 T3 aluminum is 42,000 PSI stress ratio $= \dfrac{18648}{42,000} = .444$. Margin of safety $= \dfrac{1}{.444} - 1 = 1.25$

Note: If the margin of safety is greater than *zero*, the strength is satisfactory for statically loaded parts.

One other aspect of Section A-A should be checked. This is the bearing, or crushing effect of the bolt on the .040 aluminum torques. The action here would be the elongation of the hole by "piling up" the metal on the outboard edge of the hole by cold flow.

Area of contact of *one* fork with the retention bolt is:

$$A = (.25)\ (.040) = .010\ in^2$$

$$\text{Stress (including SCF)} = \frac{(3)\ (92)}{.01} = 27,600\ PSI$$

$$\text{Stress ratio} = \frac{27,600}{64,000} = .431$$

$$\text{Margin of safety} = \frac{1}{.431} - 1 = 1.32$$

Consider Section B-B from Fig. C-1 (Fig. C-3). From a visual comparison of the area of the upper and lower plates of the fork assy. at Sections A-A versus B-B, it is obvious that B-B has the greater area of the two. Because the Section A-A has a positive margin of

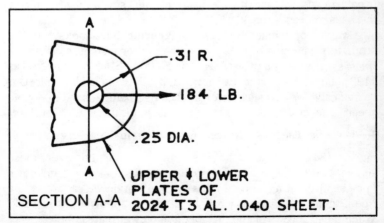

SECTION A-A

.31 R.

184 LB.

.25 DIA.

UPPER & LOWER PLATES OF 2024 T3 AL. .040 SHEET.

Fig. C-2. Section A-A. This examines the blade fork (or movable hub) at the blade retention point. The question to be answered is whether section A-A can safely stand the inflight forces imposed on it.

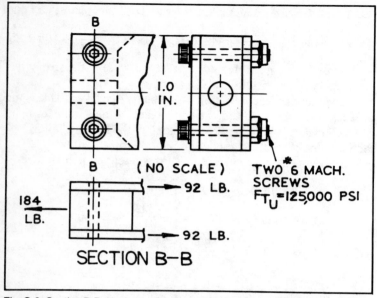

Fig. C-3. Section B-B. Here we look at the blade fork plates (top and bottom) and also the strength requirements of the #6 machine screws.

safety, it follows that B-B would also be sufficiently strong. The only part in question at B-B are the clamping bolts. Let's look at these. The sketch calls for two #6 machine screws (125,000 PSI ultimate tensile strength). To assure that you are getting good steel in bolts or screws, use the internal wrenching screw type (requiring the hexagon rod wrench).

Most good machinist or engineering handbooks list the strength properties of these as well as other fasteners. Ultimate *single shear* strength of a #6 ($F_{SU} = 125,000$ PSI) screw is listed as 1122 pounds. That is the load at which it will likely fail in shear. Our design calls for two such screws, each one being loaded in double shear. The load at each of the four shear locations is, therefore, $\frac{184}{4} = 46$ lbs. There is obviously no problem in these screws carrying the 184 lbs. in pure shear. As stated earlier, however, these screws will be required to carry the 184 lbs. *and* some unknown in-plane alternating loads. In this *one* application we can waive the rule of going to a larger screw by using the following little trick. When these screws clamp the upper and lower plates to the spacer block, the friction between the plates and the block carries the shear load. Thus we load screws in *static tension*, and because of the clamping, the friction carries the destructive alternating shear load. The conclusion is that #6 screws, used as such, are adequate.

Consider Section C-C from Fig. C-1 (Fig. C-4). Spindle bolt is made from a #10 (approx. 3/16 in. dia.) 4130 steel aircraft bolt. In threads, $F_{TY} = 50,000$ PSI. Minimum diameter in threads $= .149$ in.

$$\text{Minimum area} = \pi(\frac{.149^2}{2}) = .0174 \text{ in}^2$$

The working stress at Section C-C, including our added stress concentration factor of 3, is:

$$\text{Stress} = \frac{\text{C.F.} \times 3}{A} = \frac{(184)(3)}{.0174} = 31,724 \text{ PSI}$$

$$\text{Stress ratio} = \frac{\text{Stress}}{F_{TY}} = \frac{31,724}{50,000} = .635$$

$$\text{Margin of safety Section C-C} = \frac{1}{.635} - 1 = .574$$

We will now look at Section D-D of Fig. C-1. The area of a #10 bolt *shank* is .0283 in². The working stress at Section D-D, including our added stress concentration factor of 3 is:

$$\text{Stress} = \frac{(CF)(SCF)}{A} = \frac{(184)(3)}{.0283} = 19,505 \text{ PSI}$$

$$\text{Stress ratio} = \frac{\text{Stress}}{F_{TY}} = \frac{19,505}{82,000} = .238$$

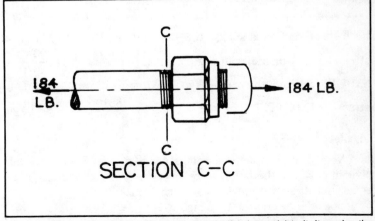

Fig. C-4. Section C-4 This is the blade spindle (feather axis) bolt. It carries the combined centrifugal (steady) load plus alternating in-plane loads.

$$\text{Margin of safety at D-D} = \frac{1}{.238} - 1 = 3.20$$

Note: Section D-D has been calculated using only the known static CF load. As previously mentioned, in forward flight, high in-plane (and flapwise with rigid rotors) loads are present, but we modelers have no reliable way to determine the magnitude of these alternating bending loads that are superimposed on the calculated static loads. Yes, the margin of safety based on the static load looks okay at Section D-D. Nevertheless, I have had one spindle of this size and material fail in the fatigue mode at Section D-D. An examination of the failed section revealed that the failure was in the in-plane (drag) direction. The conclusion, therefore, is that the 3/16 inch diameter spindle is marginal, and to avoid possible personal injury, the next larger size (.25 inch dia.) spindle would be recommended here.

Consider Section E-E of Fig. C-1. This is the blade retention bolt which, with some .40 size helicopters, would consist of not one, but two or three smaller bolts. The bolt is loaded in double shear. That is, there is a shear line between the upper tongue and the blade, and also one between the lower tongue and the blade. You may wonder why such a larger diameter bolt (¼ inch) is used here. There are two influencing factors, neither of which has to do with the bolt. First, the bearing strength in the .040 aluminum torques (resistance to hole elongation due to cold flow) is much better with larger diameter contact with the bolt. Second, the wood in the blades is less likely to be crushed in bearing by the larger bolt. To reduce weight, the bolt can be easily made from 2024 T3 aluminum bar stock. The area of the ¼ inch bolt $= \pi R^2 = \pi (.125)^2 = .049 \text{ in}^2$. Each shear section is subject to $\frac{180}{2} = 90$ lbs. The working shear stress for a ¼ inch diameter 2024 T3 *aluminum* bolt is $\frac{(90)(3)}{.049} = 5510$ PSI. From the table, the maximum allowable working stress is 40,000 PSI. The stress ration is $\frac{5510}{40,000} = .138$ Margin of safety $= \frac{1}{.138} - 1 = 6.25$.

Note: If more than one bolt is used, the load can be evenly divided between the bolts. In reality, the load distribution is not equal, but it is close enough for our purpose.

Consider Section F-F of Fig. C-1.

Blade details
Blade material: white pine (dry).

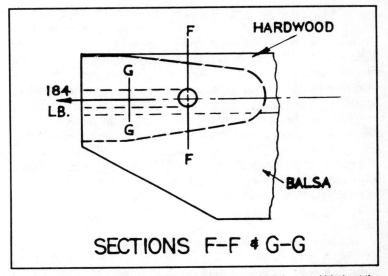

Fig. C-5. Section F-F & G-G. This looks at the strength of the wood blade at the retention bolt F-F. Will the CF crush the wood in the hole? This we determine. Last, we consider the possibility of the blade wood pulling the bolt out by double shear along the dotted lines.

> Blade chord: 2 inches.
> Airfoil: NACA 0015 (15% thickness).
> Blade thickness: (2) (.15) = .30 inch.
> Retention hole: .25 diameter (as above).

Here we will examine blade retention from the standpoint of the wood. The failure mode at Section F-F, if occurring, would be crushing in the retention hole.

The working stress, including our stress concentration factor, is:

$$\frac{3 \times CF}{A} = \frac{(3)(184)}{(.25)(.30)} = 7360 \text{ PSI}$$

$$\text{Stress ratio} = \frac{7360}{2800} = 2.63$$

$$\text{Margin of safety} = \frac{1}{2.63} - 1 = .62 \text{ (not good)}.$$

This margin of safety indicates that it would be prudent to make a design change here. The solution to the problem has several alternatives including larger retention bolt, more than one bolt, a two-piece blade with a hardwood leading edge and a balsa trailing edge (as shown in Section F-F), or ⅛ inch birch plywood doublers on the top and bottom of the blade root end (with the approximate shape as shown by the dotted line in Section F-F and G-G). The designer, at this stage, would do well to carefully review all the practical options even to the point of calculating the margins of safety resulting from *each* configuration before making a final decision.

Consider Section G-G of Fig. C-1. This failure mode considers the double shear in the wood—that is, literally pulling the bolt (and bringing the wood with it) out of the blade by shearing along the dotted lines as shown in Section G-G. This failure is rather remote if a respectable edge margin to hole diameter ratio of about 6 is used. Let's see how this would be calculated.

Total shear area = A = (6) (.25) (.30) (2) = .90 in^2

Working shear stress = $\dfrac{(3)(184}{.90}$ = 613 PSI

Stress ratio = $\dfrac{613}{740}$ = .828 (white pine)

Margin of safety is $\dfrac{1}{.828}$ -1 = .21 (marginally acceptable).

Note: An increase of "edge margin" of from 6 to 6½ or 7 might be prudent here.

The above examples are not intended to make you into a structural expert. Instead, they are aimed at giving you reasonably sound philosophical approach and procedure whereby a design on paper can become a three-dimensional reality with confidence that the machine is not likely to fail structurally.

"We have not succeeded in answering all of our questions. Indeed, we sometimes feel that we have not completely answered any of them. The answers we have found only served to raise a whole new set of questions. In some ways we feel that we are as confused as ever, but we think we are now confused on a higher level, and about more important things."

—Author unknown

Index

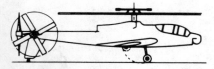

Edited by Steven Mesner